MW01258977

I Believe:
40 Daily Readings
for the Purposeful Presbyterian

Alive to God in Jesus Christ

Editors
Frank T. Hainer
Mark D. Hinds
Writer
Joseph D. Small III
Art Director
Jeanne Williams
Cover Design
Rebecca Kueber

Published by Witherspoon Press, a ministry of the General Assembly Council,
Presbyterian Church (U.S.A.), 100 Witherspoon St., Louisville, Kentucky.

PRINTED IN THE UNITED STATES OF AMERICA

www.pcusa.org/witherspoon

I Believe:
40 Daily Readings
for the Purposeful Presbyterian

Alive to God in Jesus Christ

Introduction

Baptism is the central celebration of the grace of the Lord Jesus Christ, the love of God, and the communion of the Holy Spirit. From the beginning of the Christian movement, a profession of faith preceded Baptism. The church developed the Apostles' Creed as a Baptismal creed, a concise expression of the apostolic faith uniting baptized believers. Originally, candidates for Baptism were asked three questions, answering in the words of the Creed:

> Do you believe in God?
> "I believe in God the Father Almighty . . . ."
> Do you believe in Jesus Christ?
> "I believe in Jesus Christ, his only Son our Lord . . . ."
> Do you believe in the Holy Spirit?
> "I believe in the Holy Spirit, the holy catholic church . . . ."

In the contemporary church, professions of faith are still made in response to questions. For example, "Who is your Lord and Savior?" to which persons respond, "Jesus Christ is my Lord and Savior."

At Baptism, persons declare that a human being named Jesus, who lived in a particular time and place, is God's anointed one, the very presence of God among us. As the Christ, this Jesus is Lord of time and space, Savior of the world. But there is more. Christians declare, "Jesus Christ is *my* Lord and Savior." Jesus Christ is God with us, God for us. Thus, the Baptismal profession of faith says something about God, about each of us, and about how we can live God's new Way in the world.

By reading this book you have embarked on a disciplined study of the Christian doctrine of the incarnation over the next forty days. The daily readings that follow are designed for individual study and reflection. Perhaps you observe a regular devotional time during your day; these readings could provide content for that important time. For those who wish to reflect on these readings in a group setting, a small-group study guide is offered on page 77.

"JESUS Christ Is My Lord and Savior"

Day 1 Matthew 16:13–17

Now when Jesus came into the district of Caesarea Philippi, he asked his disciples, "Who do people say that the Son of Man is?" And they said, "Some say John the Baptist, but others Elijah, and still others Jeremiah or one of the prophets." He said to them, "But who do you say that I am?" Simon Peter answered, "You are the Messiah, the Son of the living God." And Jesus answered him, "Blessed are you, Simon son of Jonah! For flesh and blood has not revealed this to you, but my Father in heaven."

Prayer:

O God, fount of all wisdom,
in the humble witness of the apostle Peter
you have shown the foundation of our faith.
Give us the light of your Spirit,
that, recognizing in Jesus of Nazareth
the Son of the living God,
we may be living stones
for the building up of your holy church;
through Jesus Christ our Lord,
who lives and reigns with you in the unity of the Holy Spirit,
one God, forever and ever. Amen.[1]

---

1. *Book of Common Worship* (Louisville: Westminster/John Knox Press, 1993), 370.

iBelieve

Mary and Miriam, Jesus and Joshua

In the sixth month the angel Gabriel was sent by God to a town in Galilee called Nazareth, to a virgin engaged to a man whose name was Joseph, of the house of David. The virgin's name was Mary. And he came to her and said, "Greetings, favored one! The Lord is with you." But she was much perplexed by his words and pondered what sort of greeting this might be. The angel said to her, "Do not be afraid, Mary, for you have found favor with God. And now, you will conceive in your womb and bear a son, and you will name him Jesus."

—Luke 1:26–31

Parents choose their children's names with great care. Mothers and fathers review all of the possibilities, often changing their minds several times before deciding on the one name that seems just right. In the end, parents may name their daughters and sons after family members, or friends, or famous people, or just because they like the sound of a name. For most people, choosing a child's name is not a casual matter, but a decision of lasting consequence. The name given to a newborn child will identify a person throughout life.

Approximately two thousand years ago God sent an angel to a young woman, with a startling message: "Greetings, favored one! The Lord is with you. . . . And now, you will conceive in your womb and bear a son, and you will name him Jesus" (*Luke 1:28, 31*).

The young woman's name was Mary, the Greek form of the Hebrew "Miriam," an honored name in Israel's history. At the time of the Hebrew Exodus from Egypt, Miriam was a prophet who sang a victory song at the crossing of the Red Sea (*Ex. 15:20–21*). Israel remembered her as one of God's chosen leaders in Israel's journey from slavery to freedom: "For I brought you up from the land of Egypt, and redeemed you from the house of slavery; and I sent before you Moses, Aaron, and Miriam" (*Micah 6:4*).

Mary named her son Jesus, the Greek form of the Hebrew "Joshua," also an honored name in Israel's history. Joshua, the designated successor to Moses, led Israel across the Jordan River into the Promised Land. (The name Joshua derives from the Hebrew for "Yahweh saves.")

Both Miriam/Mary and Joshua/Jesus were common names in first-century Palestine. They recalled great figures from Israel's history, a woman and a man who had been faithful servants of God, instruments of God's salvation. The early church understood that in Mary's son Jesus the gracious Way of God with people had come to fulfillment. Like Miriam before her, Mary sang of God's glorious triumph (*Luke 1:46–55*); like Joshua before him, Jesus led people from slavery to freedom.

The Gospel of Jesus Christ

Now the birth of Jesus the Messiah took place in this way. When his mother Mary had been engaged to Joseph, but before they lived together, she was found to be with child from the Holy Spirit. Her husband Joseph, being a righteous man and unwilling to expose her to public disgrace, planned to dismiss her quietly. But just when he had resolved to do this, an angel of the Lord appeared to him in a dream and said, "Joseph, son of David, do not be afraid to take Mary as your wife, for the child conceived in her is from the Holy Spirit. She will bear a son, and you are to name him Jesus, for he will save his people from their sins." All this took place to fulfill what had been spoken by the Lord through the prophet: "Look, the virgin shall conceive and bear a son, and they shall name him Emmanuel," which means, "God is with us."

—Matthew 1:18–23

Jesus' story is told in four Gospels: Mark, Matthew, Luke, and John. While these Gospels tell Jesus' story, they are not biographies or histories of Jesus' life and death. Rather, they are accounts of God's salvation for all people through the life, death, and resurrection of one person, Jesus of Nazareth. The Gospels relate events not simply because they happened, but because they reveal the Way of God, and the way we can live as redeemed people.

The four New Testament Gospels are accounts of the *significance* of Jesus. Their perspectives are complementary, but not identical. This is evident in the way each Gospel opens. The earliest Gospel, Mark, says nothing about Jesus' birth. For Mark, "the beginning of the good news" is the fulfillment of the Old Testament prophecy in the preaching of John the Baptist, Jesus' Baptism, the wilderness temptations, and Jesus' essential message, "The time is fulfilled, and the kingdom of God has come near; repent, and believe in the good news" (*Mark 1:15*).

Matthew and Luke, on the other hand, are very interested in Jesus' nativity, although for different reasons. Only Luke recounts the announcement to the shepherds and their visit to Bethlehem to see the newborn child. Luke's narrative of the poor, lowly outsiders signals his concern to proclaim the significance of Jesus for all who are poor and powerless. On the other hand, only Matthew recounts the story of the Magi. His narrative of the Gentiles' search for the "King of the Jews" signals Matthew's concern to proclaim the universal significance of Jesus for Jews and Gentiles. John's Gospel has no nativity narrative, opening instead with a magnificent hymn proclaiming the glory of the Word made flesh.

Although our Christmas celebrations merge Matthew and Luke into a "biographical" unity, the four Gospels display diverse, complementary proclamations of the meaning of "Emmanuel," God with us (*Matt. 1:23*). The New Testament is not indifferent to "what really happened," but its main concern is to proclaim the significance of what happened rather than to provide a chronology of Jesus' life. The Gospels are *interpretations* of the life of Jesus, not historical biographies. But the Gospels are interpretations of *the life of Jesus*, not fabrications of the early church. Mark, Matthew, Luke, and John provide us with reliable proclamations of Joshua the Messiah, Jesus Christ.

Then they brought to him a demoniac who was blind and mute; and he cured him, so that the one who had been mute could speak and see. All the crowds were amazed and said, "Can this be the Son of David?" But when the Pharisees heard it, they said, "It is only by Beelzebul, the ruler of the demons, that this fellow casts out the demons." He knew what they were thinking and said to them, "Every kingdom divided against itself is laid waste, and no city or house divided against itself will stand. If Satan casts out Satan, he is divided against himself; how then will his kingdom stand? If I cast out demons by Beelzebul, by whom do your own exorcists cast them out? Therefore they will be your judges. But if it is by the Spirit of God that I cast out demons, then the kingdom of God has come to you."
—*Matthew 12:22–28*

Throughout the Gospels, Jesus elicits response from people. The presence of Jesus and the reactions to his presence are not merely historical accounts, however. Contemporary readers and hearers are also called to make their own response.

Although there are obvious differences in emphasis and tone among the Gospels, all relate a ministry of Jesus that is grounded in the faith of Israel and marked by teaching and healing—a ministry that proclaims the good news of God's reign and offers wholeness to humankind. A "new thing" happens in Jesus' words and deeds, but it is never compellingly obvious, as if all who hear and see acknowledge the presence of God's new Way in the world. The presence of Jesus calls for decision; his words and deeds demand a response. What is true within the Gospel narratives remains true. We, too, respond and we, too, must decide. Has the Way of God drawn near in this Jesus? If so, what is the shape of God's reign? Will we choose to live within it?

Numerous healing narratives in the Gospels call out for response. A decision must be made—not about the possibility of the miraculous, but about the one who performs the miracles. The necessity of response is apparent in the healing of a "demoniac . . . blind and mute" in Matthew 12:22–28. A man who could neither see nor speak was brought to Jesus. With a dramatic economy of words, Matthew states simply, "and he cured him." What was the reaction to this wonder-filled healing? Some people asked a question, "Can this be the Son of David?" Their response was not a declaration of faith—"This is the Son of David"—but a question. Others had a quite different reaction, however, and theirs *was* a declaration: "It is only by Beelzebul, the ruler of the demons, that this fellow casts out the demons." Here, as throughout the Gospels, it is impossible not to respond. Do Jesus' actions open up God's Way in the world? Or do they present a mistaken picture of God's reign; or worse, a deceitful picture? Matthew's Gospel relates the negative response clearly, while only hinting at the positive response. The narrative leaves the question open for our own response.

Jesus' words also present occasion for decision. Parables are a characteristic form of Jesus' teaching, presenting the possibilities of God's new Way in the world. Jesus told stories about everyday realities involving laborers, bosses, merchants, neighbors, rulers, and other familiar figures. Yet into the midst of everydayness a jarring element intrudes, compelling our attention. What shepherd in his right mind would abandon his flock in search for one lost sheep? What faithful Jewish woman would put yeast in Passover bread? What sensible farmer would throw his seed on paths and rocks? These stories display something of God's Way in the world, but what is it? And what are we supposed to do? Little wonder that even those with ears to hear did not always know what to make of Jesus' teaching.

Another characteristic of Jesus' ministry was his practice of eating and drinking with all sorts of people, from the anonymous thousands, to tax collectors, to Pharisees, to just plain "sinners." What was the response to Jesus' indiscriminate eating and drinking? Some accused him of drunkenness and gluttony; many hated him for violating the bounds of covenantal observance. Others, like Zacchaeus, found salvation in Jesus' open hospitality.

Death and Life

From that time on, Jesus began to show his disciples that he must go to Jerusalem and undergo great suffering at the hands of the elders and chief priests and scribes, and be killed, and on the third day be raised. And Peter took him aside and began to rebuke him, saying, "God forbid it, Lord! This must never happen to you." But he turned and said to Peter, "Get behind me, Satan! You are a stumbling block to me; for you are setting your mind not on divine things but on human things."
—Matthew 16:21–23

The Gospels proceed from accounts of Jesus' words and deeds to extended narratives of his suffering and death. In agonizing detail they present Jesus' passion, not as the tragic end of a teacher and healer, but as the consequence and climax of his teaching and healing. The overriding response to Jesus was to kill him!

Even Jesus' resurrection—God's startling vindication of Jesus' ministry—did not evoke uniform response. The Gospels narrate the resurrection story differently, from Mark's disturbingly open-ended account to the more fully developed versions of Matthew, Luke, and John. Nevertheless, all the Gospels agree on this central point: the crucified Jesus has been raised from death to new life. But responses to this reality range through fear, doubt, disbelief, ridicule, amazement, understanding, joy, love, and worship.

As with Jesus' words and deeds, his death and resurrection demand a response and require a decision. Jesus' question "[W]ho do you say that I am?" is meant as much for us as for Peter. (See *Matt. 16:15.* It is worth noting that although Peter gave the right answer, the necessity of response did not come to an end. Peter was called upon again and again to respond, and he didn't always get it right.)

What are we to make of the Jesus we encounter in the Scriptures? On the one hand, we are not given an "objective" Jesus, but a challenge to customary ideas about God, people, the world, and the shape of faithful living. On the other hand, we are not presented with "a riddle wrapped in a mystery inside an enigma,"[1] but with reliable testimony to the presence of Emmanuel, God with us. The New Testament proclaims the significance of Jesus Christ, inviting us to answer who we say that he is, beckoning us to trust that Jesus is good news about God and God's Way among us.

---

1. Winston Churchill, as quoted in *Bartlett's Familiar Quotations*, 17th ed. (Boston: Little, Brown and Company, 2002), 665.

iBelieve

Crafting Jesus in Our Image

Now among those who went up to worship at the festival were some Greeks. They came to Philip, who was from Bethsaida in Galilee, and said to him, "Sir, we wish to see Jesus."

—John 12:20–21

In the nineteenth century, scholars set out to recover "the historical Jesus." Using the insights and techniques of modern historical scholarship, they attempted to free Jesus from the constraints of church dogma. Their aim was to present an objective "life of Jesus" that would stand the test of historical scrutiny. But Albert Schweitzer, a profound biblical scholar before he devoted his life to humanitarian work in Africa, unmasked the illusions of historical scholarship. In his book *The Quest of the Historical Jesus,* Schweitzer demonstrated that the so-called historical Jesus of nineteenth-century biographies was really a modernization, a Jesus created in the image of the times, conforming to standards of bourgeois respectability and polite morality.

Before we are too hard on the nineteenth-century quest of the historical Jesus, we must admit that the danger of crafting a Jesus in our own image is not confined to past centuries or to academic historians. The danger is clear and ever-present among us all. The Sunday school "gentle Jesus, meek and mild," the suburban "Jesus the caring helper," the Central American "Jesus the revolutionary liberator," and any number of other Jesuses may be nothing more than our own constructions, forcing the "historical Jesus" into the mold of our own preferences and needs.

But since the Gospels themselves are interpretations of the significance of Jesus, what assurance do we have that they are not mere projections of the preferences and needs of the early Christian community? A number of scholars assert that because the Gospels are interpretations by early Christian communities, we have no access to the real Jesus of history. All we have, they say, is the proclamation of the early church. Since the Gospels are particular responses to Jesus, we cannot get behind the responses to the actual Jesus of Nazareth.

Clearly, the Gospels are interpretations of the significance of Jesus. They represent responses of faith. Yet these responses of faith are built on the conviction that God's new Way had come near in the historical reality of Jesus of Nazareth. The Gospels are interpretations of something real, proclamations proceeding from reliable memory. The early church did not fabricate Jesus' words and actions in order to ground its faith. Where would that faith have come from in the first place, if not from the actual experiences and reliable memory of the life and teaching of Jesus?

That You May Come to Believe

> *Now Jesus did many other signs in the presence of his disciples, which are not written in this book. But these are written so that you may come to believe that Jesus is the Messiah, the Son of God, and that through believing you may have life in his name.*
>
> —*John 20:30–31*

Luke's Gospel follows the narrative of Jesus' nativity with accounts of his Baptism, the temptations in the wilderness, and various healings and teachings. At that point, Luke relates a visit to Jesus by disciples of John the Baptist. They ask a pointed question: "Are you the one who is to come, or are we to wait for another?" (*Luke 7:19*). That, of course, is our question as well. Is Jesus the one? Is Jesus the one in whom God has come near, in whom God makes present God's Way in the world? Do the actions and words of Jesus project before us God's new world, and will we choose to live in that new Way?

The Gospels were written "that you may come to believe that Jesus is the Messiah [Christ], the Son of God, and that through believing you may have life in his name" (*John 20:31*). We are Christians if we believe that God's Way is disclosed in the person of Jesus, and if we live this Way within a new community of discipleship. Our response to Jesus is not static, and our separate interpretations of the significance of Jesus are not identical. We are confronted again and again with the life, teachings, death, and resurrection of Jesus; again and again we are called to respond to the presence of God with us. Since our responses do not occur in isolation from the responses of other believers, but within a community of faith, we discover that interpretations of the significance of Jesus vary. The viewpoints of others may enrich our understanding, rescuing us from the danger of seeing only what we want to see. Other perspectives may also appear mistaken, but even they can sharpen our own vision.

NOTES:

"Jesus CHRIST Is My Lord and Savior"

Day 8 Philippians 2:6–11

Jesus Christ, who, though he was in the form of God,
   did not regard equality with God
   as something to be exploited,
but emptied himself,
   taking the form of a slave,
   being born in human likeness.
And being found in human form,
   he humbled himself
   and became obedient to the point of death
   —even death on a cross.
Therefore God also highly exalted him
   and gave him the name
   that is above every name,
so that at the name of Jesus
   every knee should bend,
   in heaven and on earth and under the earth,
and every tongue should confess
   that Jesus Christ is Lord,
   to the glory of God the Father.

From the Nicene Creed:
We believe in one Lord, Jesus Christ . . .
For us and for our salvation
he came down from heaven,
was incarnate of the Holy Spirit and the Virgin Mary
and became truly human.
For our sake he was crucified under Pontius Pilate;
he suffered death and was buried.
On the third day he rose again
in accordance with the Scriptures;
he ascended into heaven
and is seated at the right hand of the Father.
He will come again in glory to judge the living and the dead,
and his kingdom will have no end.[1]

1. *Book of Common Worship* (Louisville: Westminster/John Knox Press, 1993), 64.

A Confession of Faith

Jesus went on with his disciples to the villages of Caesarea Philippi; and on the way he asked his disciples, "Who do people say that I am?" And they answered him, "John the Baptist; and others, Elijah; and still others, one of the prophets." He asked them, "But who do you say that I am?" Peter answered him, "You are the Messiah."

—Mark 8:27–29

Jesus Christ: The two words are so inseparable that we may forgive children if they think "Christ" is Jesus' last name. "Christ" is not a name, of course; it is a confession of faith. "[W]ho do you say that I am?" Jesus asked Peter. Peter replied, "You are the Messiah [the Christ]" (*Mark 8:29*). *Christos,* the Greek word for the Hebrew *meshiach,* is the foundational confession of faith recorded in the Gospels. There are other confessions of faith in Jesus—Jesus is Son of God, Son of Man, Word of God, High Priest, and so on—but the confession "Messiah/Christ" is a central affirmation of the earliest Christian community.

On the surface it may appear that the Gospels tell the story of Jesus, while the rest of the New Testament proclaims Christ. Characteristically, the four Gospels refer to "Jesus," while the rest of the New Testament speaks of "Jesus Christ." Moreover, the Gospels narrate the life and teachings of Jesus, while the rest of the New Testament focuses on the significance of the crucifixion and resurrection, virtually ignoring Jesus' words and deeds. Paul goes as far as to say, "[E]ven though we once knew Christ from a human point of view, we know him no longer in that way" (*2 Cor. 5:16*).

This obvious difference in perspective has led some to separate the "simple message" of Jesus found in the Gospels from the early church's "elaborated theology" of Christ. This contrast does not accurately represent either the Gospels or the New Testament letters, however. Both Gospels and letters disclose the significance of Jesus Christ. Although different types of New Testament writings approach the reality of Jesus Christ in distinctive ways, the whole New Testament is unified in its affirmation that the human Jesus and the risen Christ are one.

> *"And now, friends, I know that you acted in ignorance, as did also your rulers. In this way God fulfilled what he had foretold through all the prophets, that his Messiah would suffer. Repent therefore, and turn to God so that your sins may be wiped out, so that times of refreshing may come from the presence of the Lord, and that he may send the Messiah appointed for you, that is, Jesus, who must remain in heaven until the time of universal restoration that God announced long ago through his holy prophets."*
>
> —Acts 3:17–21

Peter's startling confession that Jesus is the Messiah/Christ expressed the conviction that Israel's messianic hopes had found their fulfillment in Jesus. A small group of Jews came to believe that Jesus was the embodiment of God's Way, the drawing near of God's reign in the world.

Israel's messianic hopes developed over a long period. "Messiah" was a fluid hope because different groups of Jews expected God to act differently. In first-century Palestine, hope in God's salvation ranged from the expectation of national deliverance to the anticipation of spiritual purification. The Gospels themselves indicate that "messiah" was easily misunderstood and that Jesus was aware of the danger of identifying his mission with the religious and political aspirations often associated with messianic hope.

The root meaning of *messiah* is "anointed one." Whatever the form of Israel's messianic hope, the "messiah" was God's anointed, the one chosen by God to inaugurate God's rule. Peter's confession expresses the trust that Jesus is God's anointed.

Following Pentecost, Peter preached in Jerusalem about "the Messiah appointed for you, that is, Jesus" (*Acts 3:20*). Peter and the other disciples knew Jesus as the Messiah, the fulfillment of the law and the prophets, God's promised salvation. Yet, as the good news spread beyond the boundaries of Judaism into the Gentile world, the significance of "messiah" receded into the background. "Messiah" was a familiar way of expressing God's Way within

Jewish faith and life, but it was an obscure reference among Gentiles. Nevertheless, although the specifically Jewish form of messianic hope was superseded by a wider human fulfillment, Messiah/Christ remained the foundational expression of the belief that God's Way is found in Jesus. The confession that Jesus is the Messiah/Christ was so central that "Jesus Christ" (or "Christ Jesus") became inseparable in the Christian community, a "double name" that was necessary to express the reality of God with us.

Apart from a few significant passages, such as Peter's confession, Jesus is not called "Messiah/Christ" in the Gospels. In the rest of the New Testament, however, "Christ" is the customary way of referring to Jesus. This difference attests to the historical and theological reality that Jesus is fully revealed as Messiah/Christ by God's raising him from death. Jesus as the Messiah/Christ can be comprehended fully only in light of crucifixion and resurrection. Apart from the death of Jesus, the character of Jesus' messiahship could be misunderstood as a nationalistic and political phenomenon. Apart from his resurrection, Jesus would have been only one more messianic pretender. Crucifixion-resurrection is the climactic anointing of Jesus as the Messiah/Christ. The Jesus who was killed is the risen, living one; the risen, living one is the same Jesus who was crucified. Wherever we look in the New Testament—whether at Gospels or letters, at confessional formulas, worship, preaching, or mission— the central affirmation is that the human Jesus and the risen Christ are one: Jesus Christ.

The "Christ hymn" in Philippians 2:6–11 is a bold proclamation of the unified reality. The hymn expresses eloquently the significance of the life, death, and resurrection of Jesus the Christ. He was one with us, even to the point of death. Because of his absolute identification with human life, God raised him from the dead. The crucified Jesus is the risen Christ; the risen Christ is the crucified Jesus. One makes no Christian sense apart from the other.

$\mathcal{D}$ay 11   Divorcing Jesus and Christ

By this you know the Spirit of God: every spirit that confesses that Jesus Christ has come in the flesh is from God, and every spirit that does not confess Jesus is not from God.

—1 John 4:2–3

It is not uncommon for Jesus Christ to be split apart. Some see Jesus as a revered teacher who said many wise things about God and life, but not as the risen, living Christ. Others see the risen Christ as the present power of God, yet disconnected from the Jesus of Nazareth who lived and died in Palestine. Divorcing Jesus and Christ is an old temptation. Within the New Testament itself there is evidence of the struggle to maintain the essential continuity between the Jesus of history and the risen Christ who is present within the community of faith. In Hebrews we find an explicit attempt to counter overemphasis on the Jesus of history by asserting Jesus' superiority over angels, Moses, and all priests. Jesus Christ is more than messenger, prophet, or priest; Jesus Christ is "the reflection of God's glory and the exact imprint of God's very being . . . " (*Heb. 1:3*).

In the letters of John, we can see an explicit attempt to counter overemphasis on the risen Christ by asserting the reality of incarnation. "Many deceivers have gone out into the world," writes John, "those who do not confess that Jesus Christ has come in the flesh" (*2 John 7*). John is firm in stating that we can know the truth only by recognizing that "every spirit that confesses that Jesus Christ has come in the flesh is from God, and every spirit that does not confess Jesus is not from God" (*1 John 4:2–3*). The struggle within the New Testament to maintain the unity of the human Jesus and the risen Christ testifies to the centrality of that unity for Christian faith and life.

Two of the earliest Christian heresies—mistaken understandings of the gospel—are Ebionitism and Docetism. The Ebionites claimed that Jesus was simply a human being, a prophet like Moses and the other prophets. Docetists claimed that Christ was a divine being who only appeared to be human. Confronted by these one-sided views of Jesus Christ, the church had to clarify faith so that there would be no misunderstanding of the inseparable reality: Jesus Christ. In the fourth century, the Nicene Creed preserved the biblical testimony that the crucified Jesus and the risen Christ are one and the same. (See Day 8.)

One-sided views of Jesus Christ are not confined to early Christian history. Within the contemporary church there are ample instances of exclusive focus on the Jesus of history or on the risen Christ. Some within the church look to "the Jesus of the Gospels" as an example of inclusive love who provides a model for human compassion and justice. The significance of crucifixion-resurrection is slighted, or even denied. Yet disregarding the cosmic reality of the living Christ reduces Jesus to a figure from the distant past whose relevance to contemporary life is remote. Why, if Jesus is not the risen, living Christ of God, should he be our moral exemplar rather than Confucius, Mohammed, Gandhi, or George Washington? Even if we prefer the moral leadership of Jesus to that of others, what power does a long-ago and faraway Jesus have to transform our lives?

Others in the church look to "the living Christ" as a powerful presence who can provide resources for the achievement of abundant life. Jesus' human life is seen as a mere prelude to his saving death and resurrection, or even as an embarrassment. Yet this reduces Jesus Christ to a timeless abstraction that soon becomes a self-centered projection of our own desires. Maintaining the unity of Jesus Christ is a continuing task of the Christian community if it is to proclaim faithfully the good news of God's Way rather than the tired tale of our own ways.

Day 12 | Jesus Christ, the Icon of God

Therefore, since it is by God's mercy that we are engaged in this ministry, we do not lose heart. We have renounced the shameful things that one hides; we refuse to practice cunning or to falsify God's word; but by the open statement of the truth we commend ourselves to the conscience of everyone in the sight of God. And even if our gospel is veiled, it is veiled to those who are perishing. In their case the god of this world has blinded the minds of the unbelievers, to keep them from seeing the light of the gospel of the glory of Christ, who is the image of God. For we do not proclaim ourselves; we proclaim Jesus Christ as Lord and ourselves as your slaves for Jesus' sake. For it is the God who said, "Let light shine out of darkness," who has shone in our hearts to give the light of the knowledge of the glory of God in the face of Jesus Christ.

—2 Corinthians 4:1–6

Central to the faith and life of Eastern Orthodox Christians are icons, paintings, or mosaics of biblical scenes, Jesus Christ, and saints of the church. In Orthodox piety, icons are more than illustrations; they represent the truth of the thing depicted. The Greek word *eikon,* often translated "image," means a visible manifestation of reality.

Two bold passages in the New Testament identify Jesus Christ as "the icon of God," the visible manifestation of the reality of God. John's Gospel proclaims, "[T]he Word became flesh and lived among us, and we have seen his glory, the glory as of a father's only son, full of grace and truth. . . . No one has ever seen God. It is God the only Son, who is close to the Father's heart, who has made him known" (*John 1:14, 18*). The letter to the Colossians proclaims that Jesus Christ is "the image [*eikon*] of the invisible God . . . . For in him all the fullness of God was pleased to dwell" (*Col. 1:15, 19*).

God is a mystery, we sometimes say, an unknowable reality beyond all human attempts at comprehending. The "otherness" of God is not a modern discovery, however. Isaiah spoke the work of the Lord centuries ago:

For my thoughts are not your thoughts,
        nor are your ways my ways, says the Lord.
For as the heavens are higher than the earth,
        so are my ways higher than your ways
        and my thoughts than your thoughts.
                            —Isaiah 55:8–9

The good news is that God does not remain above us, cloaked in dark mystery beyond our comprehension. The gospel of Jesus Christ is the proclamation of God's nearness. Paul illuminates this gospel when he declares, "It is the God who said, 'Let light shine out of darkness,' who has shone in our hearts to give the light of the knowledge of the glory of God in the face of Jesus Christ" (2 Cor. 4:6). Jesus Christ is the icon of God, the one who shows God truly.

Day 13 In the Cross of Christ, I Glory

When I came to you, brothers and sisters, I did not come proclaiming the mystery of God to you in lofty words or wisdom. For I decided to know nothing among you except Jesus Christ, and him crucified. And I came to you in weakness and in fear and in much trembling. My speech and my proclamation were not with plausible words of wisdom, but with a demonstration of the Spirit and of power, so that your faith might rest not on human wisdom but on the power of God.

—1 Corinthians 2:1–5

What do we see when we look into the face of Jesus Christ? We see the loving God who became one with us in a life, in a death, and in a new life. We see who God is in the transforming words and actions of Jesus Christ. We see who God is on the cross of Jesus Christ. We see who God is in Jesus Christ's resurrection triumph over sin and death. We see who God is in the living presence of Jesus Christ within the community of faith. We have never seen God, but we see Jesus Christ, who makes God known.

We see God most clearly in the crucifixion of Jesus Christ. The cross is the lens through which everything else comes into focus. What Jesus said and did is understood only when viewed in retrospect from the cross. The living presence of the risen Christ is understood only in projection from the cross. "For I decided to know nothing among you," Paul wrote to the Corinthians, "except Jesus Christ, and him crucified" (*1 Cor. 2:2*). Jesus Christ is all we need to know, and we know Jesus Christ only as we know him crucified.

Paul recognized that the cross was a scandal to some, and foolishness to others. We contemporary Christians imagine that Paul was speaking about other people—"Jews and Greeks"—but not about us. Who among us doubts the centrality of the cross? Crosses adorn our churches and hang around our necks as recognizable symbols of Christian faith. Yet, in spite of the familiar presence of the cross in Christian faith and life—or perhaps because of it—we must ask ourselves if the cross of Christ has been emptied of its power (*1 Cor. 1:17*).

> *But God proves his love for us in that while we still were sinners Christ*
> *died for us. Much more surely then, now that we have been justified by*
> *his blood, will we be saved through him from the wrath of God. For if*
> *while we were enemies, we were reconciled to God through the death of*
> *his Son, much more surely, having been reconciled, will we be saved by*
> *his life. But more than that, we even boast in God through our Lord Jesus*
> *Christ, through whom we have now received reconciliation.*
>
> *—Romans 5:8–11*

Protestant crosses are literally empty. Unlike the crucifixes of
Roman Catholic Christians, our crosses do not bear the body of the
dead Jesus. Before we too quickly reply that our crosses are empty
because Christ is risen, we should acknowledge our religious
preference for resurrection victory over crucifixion suffering. We
are partial to the inspiration of joy and hope; we are put off by
immersion in sin and death. That may be why the crosses in our
churches are attractive symbols crafted in silver, unblemished by
unsightly reminders of a bloody death. We crowd into worship on
Easter, but stay far away on Good Friday.

A cross scrubbed clean from unpleasant reminders of suffering
and death can become the symbol of a disembodied Christ. In the
actual, embodied Jesus Christ, ". . . God proves his love for us in
that while we still were sinners Christ died for us. . . . For if while
we were enemies, we were reconciled to God through the death of
his Son, much more surely, having been reconciled, will we be
saved by his life" (*Rom. 5:8, 10*). Resurrection hope is empty when
it is divorced from crucifixion death.

How does the death of Jesus Christ bring about God's Way in
the world? There is no simple answer, not because crucifixion and
resurrection are perplexing riddles, but because the depth of God's
love cannot be captured in a formula.

God's Way is made known in the icon of God, Jesus Christ; the image of God in our midst is the crucified Jesus Christ. In the light of the cross, we can see clearly the significance of Jesus' life for our own lives. In the light of the cross, we can see clearly the presence of the risen Christ among us. The cross makes God known to us, reconciling us to God and to one another, forming us into the body of Christ that can now live God's Way in the world.

"Jesus Christ Is My LORD and Savior"

1 Corinthians 1:18–31

For the message about the cross is foolishness to those who are perishing, but to us who are being saved it is the power of God. For it is written,

"I will destroy the wisdom of the wise,
and the discernment of the discerning I will thwart."

Where is the one who is wise? Where is the scribe? Where is the debater of this age? Has not God made foolish the wisdom of the world? For since, in the wisdom of God, the world did not know God through wisdom, God decided, through the foolishness of our proclamation, to save those who believe. For Jews demand signs and Greeks desire wisdom, but we proclaim Christ crucified, a stumbling block to Jews and foolishness to Gentiles, but to those who are the called, both Jews and Greeks, Christ the power of God and the wisdom of God. For God's foolishness is wiser than human wisdom, and God's weakness is stronger than human strength.

Consider your own call, brothers and sisters: not many of you were wise by human standards, not many were powerful, not many were of noble birth. But God chose what is foolish in the world to shame the wise; God chose what is weak in the world to shame the strong; God chose what is low and despised in the world, things that are not, to reduce to nothing things that are, so that no one might boast in the presence of God. He is the source of your life in Christ Jesus, who became for us wisdom from God, and righteousness and sanctification and redemption, in order that, as it is written, "Let the one who boasts, boast in the Lord."

My Lord and My God

Then Paul stood in front of the Areopagus and said, "Athenians, I see how extremely religious you are in every way. For as I went through the city and looked carefully at the objects of your worship, I found among them an altar with the inscription, 'To an unknown god.' What therefore you worship as unknown, this I proclaim to you. The God who made the world and everything in it, he who is Lord of heaven and earth, does not live in shrines made by human hands."

—Acts 17:22–24

Just as Jesus Christ is an inseparable "double name," so the title "Lord" seems to be linked securely to Jesus Christ. Ordinary Christian conversation easily refers to "the Lord" when speaking about Jesus Christ, making the two virtually synonymous. "The Lord Jesus Christ" has been a customary formulation among believers from the outset of the Christian movement: the oldest New Testament letter begins with greetings "To the church of the Thessalonians in God the Father and the Lord Jesus Christ: Grace to you and peace" (*1 Thess. 1:1*). Yet "Lord" (Greek: *kurios*) is not an exclusive designation for Jesus Christ, even in the New Testament. "Lord" is first a designation for God, the triune God, not just the "second person" of the Trinity.

When Paul preached in Athens, he declared faith in "[t]he God who made the world and everything in it, he who is Lord of heaven and earth" (*Acts 17:24*). In the Revelation to John the heavenly elders sing in praise, "You are worthy, our Lord and God, to receive glory and honor and power" (*Rev. 4:11*). This identification of God as Lord reflects the faith of Israel, and can be found throughout the Old Testament. The Greek translation of the Hebrew Scriptures uses "Lord" (*kurios*) to render not only the title, *adonai*, but also the name of God, *Yahweh*. (Most English translations of the Old Testament follow the same practice: "Lord," in lowercase letters, translates the Hebrew *adonai*, while "Lord," in uppercase letters, translates the name, Yahweh.)

The New Testament also refers to the Holy Spirit as Lord: "Now the Lord is the Spirit," writes Paul, "and where Spirit of the Lord is, there is freedom" (*2 Cor. 3:17*). This early understanding of the Holy Spirit as Lord endures in the Christian community, for in the fourth-century Nicene Creed the church declared, "We believe in the Holy Spirit, the Lord, the giver of life."

God is Lord, and thus Jesus Christ is Lord, and thus the Holy Spirit is Lord. Faith in the Lord Jesus Christ is not separate from faith in "the Lord God" and "the Holy Spirit, the Lord, the giver of life."

Is "Lord" a Four-Letter Word?

. . . no one speaking by the Spirit of God ever says "Let Jesus be cursed!"
and no one can say "Jesus is Lord" except by the Holy Spirit.
—1 Corinthians 12:3

The designation "Lord," so long a fixture in Christian talk about God, has been questioned in the contemporary church. Feminist theologians have led the way in reevaluating the appropriateness of "Lord" as a way of speaking about God's self-disclosure in Jesus Christ. Their critique is important to the whole church, for it is an indictment of contemporary cultural understandings of lordship that can lead toward a recovery of the biblical witness to the sovereignty of the triune God.

The feminist critique begins with the conventional attribute of masculine gender to "Lord." Historically, the word is associated with the male-female pair of titles nobility: "lord and lady." Although this gender identification is not prominent in North American usage, it remains an instance of the church's traditional preference for using masculine images (and pronouns) for God. "Nowhere is woman's experience of male-dominated language more pervasive than in the church and synagogue," writes Letty Russell. "In hymns, liturgies, and styles of government, religious life is male-oriented."[1] Father, Son, and many other gender-specific terms reinforce the perception that "Lord" is one more in a string of exclusively masculine images for God. Even though most Christians affirm that God is beyond gender, the overwhelming use of male images, and the neglect of biblical female images, raises questions about the faithfulness of our understanding of God.

The feminist critique of "Lord" goes deeper than gender identification, however. Sallie McFague acknowledges the sense of triumph, joy, and power we feel when we hear the strains of the "Hallelujah Chorus" from Handel's *Messiah:* "King of Kings and Lord of Lords . . . the Lord God omnipotent reigneth." But

1. Letty M. Russell, *Human Liberation in a Feminist Perspective—A Theology* (Philadelphia: Westminster Press, 1974), 95.

elieve

31

she goes on to say that this powerful imaginative picture is also very dangerous, for the dualism of lord and subjects "is intrinsically hierarchical and encourages hierarchical, dualistic thinking of the sort that has fueled many kinds of oppression, including . . . those arising from the cleavages of male/female, white/colored, rich/poor, Christian/non-Christian, and mind/body."[2]

There is no doubt that everyday usage encourages an understanding of lordship that stresses the exercise of powerful domination. But is this not precisely what the lordship of God is supposed to express? Surely the Westminster Confession of Faith is correct in declaring that God is "almighty, most wise, most holy, most free, most absolute, working all things according to the counsel of his own immutable and most righteous will."[3] Surely "Lord" expresses the reality of the God who is sovereign over all creation, victorious over sin and death in Jesus Christ, the Giver of all life in the Holy Spirit. Problems arise, however, when the abstract concept of sovereign power takes precedence over biblical testimony to the grace of the Lord Jesus Christ, the love of God, and the communion of the Holy Spirit.

If we begin with a "definition" of lordship that we then apply to God, we will end up making Jesus Christ conform to cultural images of power and domination. Once we have given theological justification to social ideas about power and authority, it will seem natural—even faithful—to project hierarchical patterns onto human relationships, giving Christian support to the exercise of dominant power in the church and in society. There is no doubt that generalized ideas about lordship have been used within the church to rationalize the subjugation of women, the poor, people of color, and other "powerless" groups. Feminist theologians help the whole church to turn away from culturally conditioned religious patterns, toward the biblical witness to the Lord Jesus Christ.

2. Sallie McFague, *Models of God: Theology for an Ecological, Nuclear Age* (Philadelphia: Fortress Press, 1987), 67.
3. *The Constitution of the Presbyterian Church (U.S.A.), Part I, The Book of Confessions,* The Westminster Confession of Faith (Louisville: Office of the General Assembly), 6.011.

iBelieve

For the message about the cross is foolishness to those who are perishing, but to us who are being saved it is the power of God. For it is written, "I will destroy the wisdom of the wise, and the discernment of the discerning I will thwart."

Where is the one who is wise? Where is the scribe? Where is the debater of this age? Has not God made foolish the wisdom of the world? For since, in the wisdom of God, the world did not know God through wisdom, God decided, through the foolishness of our proclamation, to save those who believe. For Jews demand signs and Greeks desire wisdom, but we proclaim Christ crucified, a stumbling block to Jews and foolishness to Gentiles, but to those who are the called, both Jews and Greeks, Christ the power of God and the wisdom of God. For God's foolishness is wiser than human wisdom, and God's weakness is stronger than human strength.

—1 Corinthians 1:18–25

Our confession "Jesus Christ is Lord" should not proceed from the conviction that Jesus Christ fits our understanding of lordship. Rather, our understanding of "Lord" must emerge from the reality of God's self-giving in Jesus Christ. We believe in the Lord whose story is the narrative of God with us, Jesus Christ, the icon of God.

In the early church, Jesus Christ was first known as Lord through the resurrection. It is in God's raising of the crucified Jesus that Christ is confessed as Lord, the one whose name is above every name (*see Phil. 2:9–11*). But since the risen Christ is the same Jesus who lived and died, knowing the risen one as Lord means that Jesus Christ is also known as Lord in his death, his life, his Baptism, and his birth. Jesus Christ is revealed as Lord through the resurrection; yet the lordship of Jesus Christ is not only the lordship of resurrection glory, but also the lordship of crucifixion death, servant life, obedient Baptism, and ordinary birth. To confess that *Jesus Christ* is Lord is to abandon the simple cultural equation, Lord = powerful domination, and to embrace the biblical affirmation that *the Lord* is the "one who emptied himself, who took the form of a slave, who humbled himself, who became obedient, who died on an executioner's cross, and who was raised from death" (*Phil. 2:6–11*, author's translation).

Where do we see Jesus Christ the Lord? We see the Lord on the cross as surely as at the "right hand" of God. The resurrection reveals what has always been true: Jesus Christ is Lord. And in the light of resurrection we can understand "Lord" in terms of service as well as authority, humiliation as well as exaltation, friendship as well as leadership, solidarity as well as power. The Lord is not simply God above us, but with us and for us.

All of this comes to a dramatic expression in 1 Corinthians 1:18–31. The power of God, says Paul, is the message of the cross! Identifying God's power with a bloody victim of violence makes no common sense, for the message about the cross appears to be foolish talk about mortal weakness, not a wise exposition of divine power. We, like the Jews and Gentiles before us, prefer the sophisticated certainty of an omnipotent "lord," but what we get is Christ crucified. We want mighty demonstrations of divine power and profound insights into heavenly truth, but what we get is the scandal and folly of the cross. We confess that Jesus Christ is Lord, "the power of God and the wisdom of God," yet God's power and wisdom are always cruciform.

The cross turns all human standards inside out, revealing the impossible possibility that " . . . God's foolishness is wiser than human wisdom, and God's weakness is stronger than human strength" (*1 Cor. 1:25*). If Jesus Christ is Lord, then our notions of power and authority—both God's and our own—must undergo transformation by being conformed to the gospel.

> *For I am convinced that neither death, nor life, nor angels, nor rulers,*
> *nor things present, nor things to come, nor powers, nor height, nor*
> *depth, nor anything else in all creation, will be able to separate us from*
> *the love of God in Christ Jesus our Lord.*
>
> —Romans 8:38–39

God's power, revealed in the cross, is not the only power among us. The New Testament acknowledges what we know in our own lives—there are other powers in the world that dominate human life. Ideologies, institutions, modes of thought, and "lifestyles" mold our understanding of who we are, who others are in relation to us, and how we are to live. When the New Testament talks about "principalities and powers, thrones and dominions, elemental spirits,"[1] it is not engaging in mythical speculation about mysterious supernatural beings. Principalities and powers are everyday realities that seek to shape human life.

"The powers that be" in human life are known among us as "the way things are." Their power over us lies precisely in the taken-for-grantedness. People who know they are oppressed rarely embrace despotism willingly. Whether they rebel against their masters or endure in powerless resignation, human beings do not enjoy harsh tyranny. The most powerful weapon in the hands of a tyrant is not force, but the appearance of normalcy. If people do not acknowledge their oppression—because the trains run on time or because bread and circuses abound—the power of the despot is increased. There are powers over us that exercise control through our acceptance of their authority as part of what is normal in life— "the way things are."

Ideologies, patterns of thought that organize perceptions of "reality," influence the way people understand the world. Socialism, communism, capitalism, liberalism, conservatism, patriarchy, and a host of other theoretical constructions affect the ways we think and act. It is easy for us to perceive that other

---

1. See, for example, *Rom. 8:38; 1 Cor. 15:24; Eph. 1:21; 6:12;* and *Col. 2:15.*

people are captivated by "alien ideologies." But it may be difficult for them to understand their domination, and almost impossible for us to see that we, too, are in thrall to our own ideological masters.

Finally, be strong in the Lord and in the strength of his power. Put on the whole armor of God, so that you may be able to stand against the wiles of the devil. For our struggle is not against enemies of blood and flesh, but against the rulers, against the authorities, against the cosmic powers of this present darkness, against the spiritual forces of evil in the heavenly places.

—Ephesians 6:10–12

Perhaps we can understand the power of ideology among us in the North American experience of racism. Legal segregation of African Americans, for instance, was a feature of life in the United States well into the 1960s. While slavery ended with the Civil War and Reconstruction, an enduring pattern of oppression was constructed through laws that dictated separation and inequality. Throughout decades of separate schools, housing, public accommodations, and more, most white Americans comfortably accepted the ideology of segregation as the normal ordering of society. Now, most Americans look back on the days of legalized racism as a shameful period in our history. How could we have accepted so unthinkingly such a clearly evil way of life?

Thus, it is difficult to acknowledge the abiding presence of racism in American life. Many people become impatient with continuing charges of racism because they believe it is a thing of the past. "The way things are" in the United States today masks the endurance of the ideology of racism in America. The power of ideology to shape life depends on our failure to recognize it in the ongoing patterns of society.

Institutions also hold sway over us. Businesses, schools, and other organizations influence profoundly our outlook on life.

The society we live in projects images of what is "real." Advertising, entertainment, and sports cultivate powerful images of women and men, status and desirability, quality and value. Television images of beauty, violence, lifestyles, and success affect our perceptions of what is acceptable and desirable. Sports are a powerful influence on cultural norms of success and failure.

None of this means that our culture is an evil despot, or that we are unthinking pawns, unable to make meaningful decisions about our lives. It is only to say that we live within social systems of meaning that affect the ways we think and the ways we act. Our understanding of race, family, competition, beauty, death, morality, and more is shaped by "the way things are" in early twenty-first-century North America. Some of that may be very good indeed, but, for better or worse, we are not the exclusive rulers of our fate and captains of our soul.

Who Is Your Lord?

Therefore God also highly exalted him
and gave him the name
that is above every name,
so that at the name of Jesus
every knee should bend,
in heaven and on earth and under the earth,
and every tongue should confess
that Jesus Christ is Lord,
to the glory of God the Father.
            —Philippians 2:9–11

"Who is your Lord?" The question is about far more than religious affiliation, for it cuts to the heart of who we are and how we live. What gives focus to our vision of the way things are in the world? What provides shape to the way we live our lives?

Confessing Jesus Christ as Lord is a decision to conform our lives to God's Way in the world rather than to live in conformity to "the way things are." Jesus Christ is not a confirmation of society's values of cultural norms, but God's invitation to a new Way of living. The tension between God's Way and our ways is sometimes dramatic, more often embedded in ordinary living, and always difficult to acknowledge. The ideologies, institutions, and images that tyrannize us operate in subtle ways, disguising themselves in the cloak of commonsense reality.

When the earliest Christians declared, "Jesus Christ is Lord," it was clear to everyone that they were simultaneously denying "Caesar is lord." Their confession was not merely a choice for one leader over another, however, but a choice for God's Way in the world over the ordering of life in the universal Roman Empire. The lord Caesar stood at the head of a social system marked by power and characterized by a complex arrangement of duties and privileges. The Lord Jesus Christ beckoned women and men, slaves and free people, Jews and Gentiles, into a new, God-given Way of life. To be a Christian is to trust God's Way, joining with others to live in that Way.

In the 1930s, Adolph Hitler became Caesar in Germany. Nazi ideology, institutions, and images of "Aryans" and Jews laid claim to the total allegiance of a nation. A small group of Christians met in the town of Barmen to declare that "Jesus Christ . . . is the one Word of God which we have to hear and which we have to trust and obey in life and in death." That meant, however, that there were other words that could not be trusted and obeyed: "We reject the false doctrine, as though the church could and would have to acknowledge . . . other events and powers, figures and truths . . . . We reject the false doctrine, as though there were areas of our life in which we would not belong to Jesus Christ, but to other lords . . . ."[1]

Few Christians are faced with the dramatic choices of first-century Christians in the Roman Empire or twentieth-century Christians in the German Reich. Yet all Christians, in confessing Jesus Christ as Lord, must also renounce the sovereignty of other lords. In trusting God's Way, Christians must abandon allegiance to "the way things are."

---

1. *The Constitution of the Presbyterian Church (U.S.A.), Part I, The Book of Confessions,* The Theological Declaration of Barmen (Louisville: Office of the General Assembly), 8.10–15.

iBelieve

"Jesus Christ Is My Lord and SAVIOR"

For you are a people holy to the LORD your God; the LORD your God has chosen you out of all the peoples on earth to be his people, his treasured possession.

It was not because you were more numerous than any other people that the LORD set his heart on you and chose you—for you were the fewest of all peoples. It was because the LORD loved you and kept the oath that he swore to your ancestors, that the LORD has brought you out with a mighty hand, and redeemed you from the house of slavery, from the hand of Pharaoh king of Egypt. Know therefore that the LORD your God is God, the faithful God who maintains covenant loyalty with those who love him and keep his commandments, to a thousand generations . . . .

—Deuteronomy 7:6–9

The days are surely coming, says the LORD, when I will make a new covenant with the house of Israel and the house of Judah. It will not be like the covenant that I made with their ancestors when I took them by the hand to bring them out of the land of Egypt—a covenant that they broke, though I was their husband, says the LORD. But this is the covenant that I will make with the house of Israel after those days, says the LORD: I will put my law within them, and I will write it on their hearts; and I will be their God, and they shall be my people. No longer shall they teach one another, or say to each other, "Know theLORD," for they shall all know me, from the least of them to the greatest, says the LORD; for I will forgive their iniquity, and remember their sin no more.

—Jeremiah 31:31–34

iBelieve

I do not understand my own actions. For I do not do what I want, but I do the very thing I hate. Now if I do what I do not want, I agree that the law is good. But in fact it is no longer I that do it, but sin that dwells within me. For I know that nothing good dwells within me, that is, in my flesh. I can will what is right, but I cannot do it. For I do not do the good I want, but the evil I do not want is what I do. Now if I do what I do not want, it is no longer I that do it, but sin that dwells within me.

So I find it to be a law that when I want to do what is good, evil lies close at hand. For I delight in the law of God in my inmost self, but I see in my members another law at war with the law of my mind, making me captive to the law of sin that dwells in my members. Wretched man that I am! Who will rescue me from this body of death?

Thanks be to God through Jesus Christ our Lord! So then, with my mind I am a slave to the law of God, but with my flesh I am a slave to the law of sin.

—Romans 7:15–25

> *. . . because if you confess with your lips that Jesus is Lord and believe in your heart that God raised him from the dead, you will be saved. For one believes with the heart and so is justified, and one confesses with the mouth and so is saved. The scripture says, "No one who believes in him will be put to shame." For there is no distinction between Jew and Greek; the same Lord is Lord of all and is generous to all who call on him. For, "Everyone who calls on the name of the Lord shall be saved."*
>
>   *—Romans 10:9–13*

"Are you saved?" When we hear those words, many of us think of clumsy, overzealous attempts to badger us about our faith. The question may seem intrusive, a violation of the essential privacy of our religious convictions.

If we overcome our annoyance at the questioner's encroachment on our privacy, we may wonder: Saved from what? A standard formula usually lies behind the question "Are you saved?" Our questioner probably assumes that we, like all people, are sinners who deserve God's punishment. God is a just God, the formula goes, and our violations of God's law bring God's wrath upon us. We are under sentence of death for our transgressions, an eternity of hellish separation from God. Damnation is what we need to be saved from.

If we are convinced that we need to be saved from an eternity in hell, we may begin to ask questions: How can I be saved from such a dreadful destiny? Who will save me? What do I need to do to be saved? The standard formula is simple enough. We can be saved from eternal damnation only by the gracious love of God in Jesus Christ. The death and resurrection of Jesus Christ saved us from our sentence of death, assuring us of eternal life with God in heaven. Salvation in Christ is not automatic, however. We will be saved from our sentence of eternal death only if we believe that Christ died for us. Thus the formula concludes with the necessity of accepting Jesus Christ as our "personal Savior." How do we accept Christ as our Savior? By acknowledging our sin and inviting Jesus into our hearts.

So goes one common account of what it means to confess that Jesus Christ is Savior. Is that an adequate proclamation of the gospel? Does it express the fullness of God's grace in Jesus Christ?

Christian understanding of salvation grows from the whole biblical witness to Jesus Christ. The New Testament contains summaries of the good news such as, "The saying is sure and worthy of full acceptance, that Christ Jesus came into the world to save sinners . . . " (*1 Tim. 1:15*). However, the church's proclamation of the meaning of such summaries must grow from the full range of the Bible's witness to God's salvation in Jesus Christ. We must ensure that our formulations of the good news are faithful to the love of God, the grace of the Lord Jesus Christ, and the communion of the Holy Spirit.

Day 24 God Has Brought to Israel a Savior

*Then they asked for a king; and God gave them Saul son of Kish, a man
of the tribe of Benjamin, who reigned for forty years. When he had
removed him, he made David their king. In his testimony about him he
said, 'I have found David, son of Jesse, to be a man after my heart, who
will carry out all my wishes.' Of this man's posterity God has brought to
Israel a Savior, Jesus, as he promised.*

—*Acts 13:21–23*

The New Testament book of the Acts of the Apostles provides us
with insight into the proclamation of the earliest Christians. Acts'
accounts of preaching by Peter and Paul are not transcripts of their
sermons, but outlines of the message they proclaimed. One
narrative of Paul's preaching is set in Antioch of Pisidia, a city in
Asia Minor. When Paul and his companions visited the synagogue
to worship God, they were invited to speak. Paul's message to the
faithful was dramatic: " . . . God has brought to Israel a Savior,
Jesus, as he promised" (*Acts 13:23*).

What did Israel need to be saved from? Israel knew itself as a
people God had saved:

> For you are a people holy to the LORD your God; the LORD
> your God has chosen you out of all the peoples on earth to
> be his people, his treasured possession. It was not because
> you were more numerous than any other people that the
> LORD set his heart on you and chose you—for you were the
> fewest of all peoples. It was because the LORD loved you and
> kept the oath that he swore to your ancestors, that the LORD
> has brought you out with a mighty hand, and redeemed you
> from the house of slavery, from the hand of Pharaoh king
> of Egypt. Know therefore that the LORD your God is God,
> the faithful God who maintains covenant loyalty with those
> who love him and keep his commandments, to a thousand
> generations . . . (*Deut. 7:6–9*).

The Jews in Antioch, like Jews everywhere, knew that they did not deserve God's favor. They took no pride in being chosen by God, for they understood that God's gracious love had been freely given to an insignificant band of slave laborers and their descendants. Israel was saved by grace. Furthermore, the Jews in Antioch, like Jews everywhere, knew that they could not earn God's favor by obedience to the law. The commandments were God's gift to the people God had saved, the shape of faithful life within God's gracious Way. Obedience to the law was Israel's response to salvation, not a way to gain salvation.

Day 25 — Saved from What?

Let it be known to you therefore, my brothers, that through this man forgiveness of sins is proclaimed to you; by this Jesus everyone who believes is set free from all those sins from which you could not be freed by the law of Moses.

—*Acts 13:38–39*

So what did Israel need to be saved from? Paul's message in the Antioch synagogue was "that through this man [Jesus] forgiveness of sins is proclaimed to you; by this Jesus everyone who believes is set free from all those sins from which you could not be freed by the law of Moses" (*Acts 13:38–39*). Although the law provided the shape of faithfulness for a redeemed people, even Israel's diligent attention to fulfilling the commandments could not overcome the continuing reality of sin. God's Way was not the way of the world, not even the way of those who tried to live faithfully. The Jews in Antioch, like Jews everywhere, knew that God alone could save them from continuing slavery to sin, and that God alone could fulfill the promise of the new life. Israel could not live God's Way in the world without redemption from slavery to sin.

God's grace had saved Israel from Egyptian slavery and set Israel within God's everlasting covenant of love. Yet Israel was unable to live fully within God's righteousness. Israel lived in hope of seeing the dawn of God's salvation. God's promise, spoken through prophets, was firm:

The days are surely coming, says the LORD, when I will make a new covenant with the house of Israel and the house of Judah. It will not be like the covenant that I made with their ancestors when I took them by the hand to bring them out of the land of Egypt . . . . I will put my law within them, and will write it on their hearts; and I will be their God, and they shall be my people. . . . I will forgive their iniquity, and remember their sin no more (*Jer. 31:31–34*).

Only God's grace could save Israel from slavery to the power of sin and fulfill the promise of new life in God's Way. Now, said Paul, " . . . God has brought to Israel a Savior, Jesus, as he promised" (*Acts 13:23*). Paul's message was more than good news for Israel, however, for he went on to proclaim that God's salvation was for all people, Gentiles as well as Jews. Paul concluded his sermon in Antioch with the announcement of salvation for the world: "[T]he Lord has commanded us, saying, 'I have set you to be a light for the Gentiles, so that you may bring salvation to the ends of the earth.' " Little wonder that "When the Gentiles heard this, they were glad and praised the word of the Lord" (*Acts 13:47, 48*). In Jesus Christ, Jew and Gentile together were saved from their captivity to sin.

Day 26 Enslaved to Sin

For if we have been united with him in a death like his, we will certainly be united with him in a resurrection like his. We know that our old self was crucified with him so that the body of sin might be destroyed, and we might no longer be enslaved to sin. For whoever has died is freed from sin. But if we have died with Christ, we believe that we will also live with him. We know that Christ, being raised from the dead, will never die again; death no longer has dominion over him. The death he died, he died to sin, once for all; but the life he lives, he lives to God. So you also must consider yourselves dead to sin and alive to God in Christ Jesus.

—*Romans 6:5–11*

The mention of "sin" usually brings to mind a catalog of wrongdoings. We review our actions, both good and bad, calling the bad things we have done "sins." We may assume that God, like a stern parent, is angry with us for the bad things we have done. In order to restore God's favor, then, we must be sorry for our sin and ask for forgiveness. Of course, just like children, we know that we do good things as well as bad things. On the whole, we think of ourselves as pretty good boys and girls. We are not perfect children, but we want approval for the good things we have done, and we do not like to be blamed for bad things we have not done.

If that is our understanding of sin, it is little wonder that so many of us have trouble with prayers of confession in worship. Why should we confess sins we haven't committed? The printed words ask us to confess, "We have turned from our neighbors, and refused to bear the burdens of others. We have ignored the pain of the world, and passed by the hungry, the poor, and the oppressed."[1] Is that fair? Prayers of confession are so harsh. We know we are not faultless, but we also know that we have helped some neighbors, and given assistance to some of the hungry, the homeless, and the needy. It does not seem right that prayers of confession fail to recognize the good things we do, asking us to pray as if we were guilty of everything all the time.

1. *Book of Common Worship* (Louisville: Westminster/John Knox Press, 1993), 54.

iBelieve

We misunderstand the reality of sin if we imagine checklists that catalog good and bad deeds, right and wrong actions. Sin is far more than the debit column on a moral balance sheet. Sin is nothing less than a powerful force that turns us away from God's Way, bending us toward easy acceptance of "the way things are."

Sin's power does not twist us into the grotesque shape of moral monsters who are incapable of doing anything that is just and loving. The world knows the reality of Hitler and Pol Pot, white supremacists and terrorists, drug dealers and child abusers, but they do not define sin's power in the world. The world also knows the reality of Martin Luther King Jr. and Mother Teresa, people who work for racial harmony and peace, hospice volunteers and caring social workers, but their lives do not refute the power of sin among us.

Sin is not confined to wicked villains or absent from moral heroes. Sin's pervasive power works at the core of our very ordinary lives.

Day 27 Jesus Christ Frees Us

When you were slaves of sin, you were free in regard to righteousness.
So what advantage did you then get from the things of which you now
are ashamed? The end of those things is death. But now that you have
been freed from sin and enslaved to God, the advantage you get is
sanctification. The end is eternal life. For the wages of sin is death,
but the free gift of God is eternal life in Christ Jesus our Lord.
—Romans 6:20–23

Frederick Buechner, a novelist and theologian, has a knack for
creating images that bring abstract ideas into focus. Buechner
graphically describes the power of sin in human life:

> The power of sin is centrifugal. When at work in a human
> life, it tends to push everything out toward the periphery. Bits
> and pieces go flying off until only the core is left. Eventually
> bits and pieces of the core itself go flying off until in the end
> nothing at all is left. "The wages of sin is death" is Saint
> Paul's way of saying the same thing.[1]

Does this sound too dramatic? We do not experience ourselves
as hollow people, emptied of God, of others, of ourselves. Most of
us are quite ordinary, living lives that know joy as well as sorrow,
care as well as indifference, fulfillment as well as emptiness. Yet
although we do not experience ourselves as miserable wretches,
empty and aimless, Buechner's dramatic picture sparks a light
of recognition in us. It takes only a small measure of honesty about
ourselves to acknowledge that even the best within us can slip
off center. Our deepest, dearest relationships with family and
friends can go awry. Our most worthy goals can recede into the
background. The reality of sin is not confined to the presence of
gross evil; sin's power works its way in the ordinary journey of
everyday life, throwing us off course by slight, barely noticed
changes in direction.

1. Frederick Buechner, *Wishful Thinking: A Seeker's ABC* (San Francisco:
   HarperSanFrancisco, 1993), 108.

iBelieve

The reality of sin in our lives is pervasive, touching us all at the core of our being. Sin's centrifugal force spins us away from the center, away from God, and thus away from being the people God created us to be. We are like wobbling tops, continuing to spin, but no longer maintaining axis or position.

We are not deliberately malevolent, willfully disregarding God and other people. Yet Paul's experience is all-too-familiar: "I do not understand my own actions. For I do not do what I want, but I do the very thing I hate. . . . I can will what is right, but I cannot do it. For I do not do the good I want, but the evil I do not want is what I do" (*Rom. 7:15, 18–19*). Paul and we together understand the contradiction that lives within the heart of life. What Paul may understand better than we is that we are prisoners of forces that work against us. "Now if I do what I do not want . . . it is no longer I that do it, but sin that dwells within me" (*Rom. 7:16–17*). It is true enough that we are willing prisoners, complacent in the contradictions that confine us. Yet it is also true that sin has a hold on us that inhibits our capacity to live in harmony with God, with others, and with ourselves, even at the points where our intentions are clearest.

"Wretched man that I am!" cries Paul. "Who will rescue me from this body of death?" Who indeed! Paul's answer is good news: "Thanks be to God through Jesus Christ our Lord!" (*Rom. 7:24, 25*). Jesus Christ frees us from slavery to sin. Jesus Christ is Savior.

iBelieve

No Longer Enslaved to Sin

So we are ambassadors for Christ, since God is making his appeal through us; we entreat you on behalf of Christ, be reconciled to God. For our sake he made him to be sin who knew no sin, so that in him we might become the righteousness of God.

—*2 Corinthians 5:20–21*

As Israel was led from Egyptian bondage to the freedom of God's Promised Land, so we are rescued from slavery to sin and set within the freedom of God's grace. In Jesus Christ we are liberated from bondage to "the way things are," set free from captivity to the centrifugal force of sin.

The good news of Jesus Christ is that God does for us what we cannot do by ourselves. God has not consigned us to the ambiguity of "self-help," the constant striving to overcome the contradictions in our own lives. In the first century this meant that people no longer had to justify their own lives by constantly striving to observe the Law's details. In our time, this may mean that we do not have to gauge the worth of our lives by following the details of "self-improvement" programs. Both God's Law and all the varieties of self-help systems can be good and helpful parts of life, but neither is able to rescue us from the debilitating power of sin. For that, we need a Savior, One who can set us free from constant striving and from constant failure to achieve full communion with God and with other people.

We proclaim that Jesus Christ is Emmanuel—God with us in life, in death, and in new life. God is with us and for us to liberate us from bondage to sin and death, freeing us for life lived in God's good Way. Paul phrases the gospel of Christ's salvation in astonishing terms: "For our sake [God] made him to be sin who knew no sin, so that in him we might become the righteousness of God" (2 Cor. 5:21). Jesus Christ became one with us, enduring all the effects of human sin. Like us, he was opposed and betrayed, misunderstood and abandoned. Like us, he suffered the agonies that are too often a part of human life, including physical pain and untimely death. In all of this, he knew the temptation to forsake

God and to abandon people. Jesus Christ's absolute solidarity with our life, including our death, means oneness with us in life lived under the shadow of sin.

But Jesus' life was not just one more instance of the victory of sin and death. This one human life was lived in absolute solidarity with God as well as with us. Unqualified faithfulness to God is beyond our capacity, yet this human one, Jesus the Christ, lived a life and died a death of complete fidelity to God's Way in the world. In Jesus Christ we see what truly human life is. As Jesus Christ joins himself to us in life and death, so Jesus Christ joins us to himself in victory over sin and death.

Freedom!

NOTES:

"Jesus Christ IS MY Lord and Savior"

Day 29 Colossians 2:9–13; James 2:12–26

For in him the whole fullness of deity dwells bodily, and you have come to fullness in him, who is the head of every ruler and authority. In him also you were circumcised with a spiritual circumcision, by putting off the body of the flesh in the circumcision of Christ; when you were buried with him in Baptism, you were also raised with him through faith in the power of God, who raised him from the dead. And when you were dead in trespasses and the uncircumcision of your flesh, God made you alive together with him, when he forgave us all our trespasses.

—Colossians 2:9–13

So speak and so act as those who are to be judged by the law of liberty. For judgment will be without mercy to anyone who has shown no mercy; mercy triumphs over judgment.

What good is it, my brothers and sisters, if you say you have faith but do not have works? Can faith save you? If a brother or sister is naked and lacks daily food, and one of you says to them, "Go in peace; keep warm and eat your fill," and yet you do not supply their bodily needs, what is the good of that? So faith by itself, if it has no works, is dead.

But someone will say, "You have faith and I have works." Show me your faith apart from your works, and I by my works will show you my faith. You believe that God is one; you do well. Even the demons believe—and shudder. Do you want to be shown, you senseless person, that faith apart from works is barren? Was not our ancestor Abraham justified by works when he offered his son Isaac on the altar? You see that faith was active along with his works, and faith was brought to completion by the works. Thus the Scripture was fulfilled that says, "Abraham believed God, and it was

iBelieve

reckoned to him as righteousness," and he was called the friend of God. You see that a person is justified by works and not by faith alone. Likewise, was not Rahab the prostitute also justified by works when she welcomed the messengers and sent them out by another road? For just as the body without the spirit is dead, so faith without works is also dead.

—James 2:12–26

Hymn:

I greet Thee, who my sure Redeemer art,
My only trust and Savior of my heart,
Who pain didst undergo for my poor sake;
I pray Thee from our hearts all cares to take.

Thou art the King of mercy and of grace,
Reigning omnipotent in every place:
So come, O King, and our whole being sway;
Shine on us with the light of Thy pure day.

Thou art the life, by which alone we live,
And all our substance and our strength receive;
Sustain us by Thy faith and by Thy power,
And give us strength in every trying hour.

Thou hast the true and perfect gentleness,
No harshness hast Thou and no bitterness:
O grant to us the grace we find in Thee,
That we may dwell in perfect unity.

Our hope is in no other save in Thee;
Our faith is built upon Thy promise free;
Lord, give us peace, and make us calm and sure,
That in Thy strength we evermore endure.[1]

---

1. "I Greet Thee, Who My Sure Redeemer Art," *The Presbyterian Hymnal* (Louisville: Westminster/John Knox Press, 1990), no. 457. Attributed to John Calvin.

iBelieve

The next day the great crowd that had come to the festival heard that Jesus was coming to Jerusalem. So they took branches of palm trees and went out to meet him, shouting, "Hosanna! Blessed is the one who comes in the name of the Lord—the King of Israel!"

—John 12:12–13

"Who is your Lord and Savior?"
"Jesus Christ is my Lord and Savior!"

This central affirmation of Christian faith hinges on the two little words in the middle: "is my." Apart from them, everything else recedes into history or flies into abstraction. The word "is" places "Jesus Christ, Lord and Savior" in the present tense, while the word "my" places "Jesus Christ, Lord and Savior" in the lives of people.

The ancient Easter acclamation reverberates through the centuries: "Christ is risen! Christ is risen indeed!" Christians do not make a mere historical statement—"Christ was risen"—as if we were acknowledging an event in the distant past. To proclaim that Christ is risen is to proclaim the presence of the living Christ among us now as Lord and Savior. Christian talk about Jesus Christ occurs in the present tense. Or does it? Actually, two realities of contemporary church life conspire to relegate Jesus Christ to the past. Ironically, our Easter celebration and our study of the Bible may push the living One back into the recesses of an ancient past.

Easter is the climax of the church's "Holy Week," an eight-day progression through the Gospel narratives, from Palm Sunday through Maundy Thursday and Good Friday to Easter Sunday. While it is appropriate to maintain the gospel's grounding in the actual events of Jesus' life, our Holy Week can give the impression of transporting us back into a historical re-creation of events in Jerusalem, as if we were participating in a psychological pageant.

iBelieve

It all begins with Palm Sunday, the day of the big parade. Jesus' "triumphal entry" into Jerusalem is celebrated with songs of victory and palm fronds, sometimes with real donkeys and period costumes. We sing "Hosanna" along with the residents of first-century Palestine, pretending that we do not know what lies ahead. The cruel irony of Palm Sunday is lost in festive re-creation. (The church's efforts to call the day "Passion Sunday"—"Suffering Sunday"—have been doomed to failure.)

North American Christians skip over the next three days—the cleansing of the Temple, controversies with religious authorities, and the anointing at Bethany—in order to arrive directly in Maundy Thursday's upper room for a somber observance of the "Last" Supper. Bread and wine are shared in an atmosphere of foreboding, complete with funeral music and the extinguishing of light. Then comes "Good" Friday, a three-hour ordeal of grieving over the agonizing death of Jesus.

From the playful festivity of Palm Sunday to the somber grief of Good Friday, the church tries to recapitulate the decent into darkness, enfolding the faithful in a tragic drama. The circle is closed happily on Easter morning, however, with shouts of joy at the risen tomb. We, like the grieving, frightened disciples, listen to the wonderful message of the women: He is risen! Now we can sing glorious Easter hymns to the accompaniment of trumpets. But *what* do we celebrate?

Day 31 | Celebrate What?

But Thomas (who was called the Twin), one of the twelve, was not with them when Jesus came. So the other disciples told him, "We have seen the Lord." But he said to them, "Unless I see the mark of the nails in his hands, and put my finger in the mark of the nails and my hand in his side, I will not believe."

A week later his disciples were again in the house, and Thomas was with them. Although the doors were shut, Jesus came and stood among them and said, "Peace be with you." Then he said to Thomas, "Put your finger here and see my hands. Reach out your hand and put it in my side. Do not doubt but believe." Thomas answered him, "My Lord and my God!" Jesus said to him, "Have you believed because you have seen me? Blessed are those who have not seen and yet have come to believe."

—John 20:24–29

If all we are celebrating is a past event—the resurrection of a dead man in Palestine—it is little wonder that our best attempts to enter into Holy Week end in failure. We cannot maintain a journey through the remote past, and so most church members skip from Palm Sunday applause directly to Easter Sunday anthems, avoiding the depressing remembrance of conflict, betrayal, abandonment, and death.

Because we cannot "be there" when they crucified our Lord, our failed attempt at historical reconstruction must be replaced by some contemporary significance. Thus Easter becomes a "Rite of Spring," replete with lilies, eggs, bunnies, and our joyous welcome of the earth's rebirth! "Springtime is risen!" we seem to say. "Springtime is risen indeed!" We are disappointed if Easter Sunday is marred by cold, gray weather, and we are vaguely puzzled by Easter in the southern hemisphere, where the Day of Resurrection comes during the onset of autumn.

Too often, the church's Holy Week imprisons Jesus Christ in an inaccessible past, remote from the reality of our lives. "Easter past" is only a pointed instance of what often happens with our study of the Bible, however. Our appropriate attempts to understand the

i*B*elieve

history and culture of "Bible times" often result in an objectifying distance between us and the proclamation of the Scriptures. Bible study can deteriorate into mildly uninteresting history lessons, exercises in archaeological excavation of an alien past.

For example, study of Jesus' parables often focuses on lessons about Palestinian wedding customs and farming methods so that the bold contemporary challenge of God's Way among us now is lost in the recesses of the distant past.

Christian faith can never abandon its firm grounding in the historical reality of Jesus of Nazareth. "God with us" is not a disembodied abstraction, but a genuine presence in the reality of human life. Yet Christian faith cannot become a prisoner to the past. "God with us" is not a tale told about "long ago and far away," but a genuine presence among us now. Jesus Christ is our Lord and Savior: the One who lived and died is raised from death—the living One in our midst. Our confession of faith is not confined to the objective acknowledgment of historical fact. The living One is, now, the Lord who saves us from bondage to all that would keep us from God's Way.

[F]or in Christ Jesus you are all children of God through faith. As many of you as were baptized into Christ have clothed yourselves with Christ. There is no longer Jew or Greek, there is no longer slave or free, there is no longer male and female; for all of you are one in Christ Jesus. And if you belong to Christ, then you are Abraham's offspring, heirs according to the promise.

—Galatians 3:26–29

The risen Christ, alive among us now, is more than a vague contemporary presence. "God with us" is with us in the tangible realities of life. Some Christians express God's intimate presence by calling Jesus Christ their "personal savior," the One they have welcomed into their hearts. While this way of talking about the real presence of Christ expresses the truth of God's nearness, it runs the risk of making Jesus Christ into the private possession of individual believers.

The New Testament puts matters somewhat differently. Paul speaks repeatedly of our being "in Christ," rather than of Christ being "in me." "So if anyone is in Christ," says Paul, "there is a new creation" (*2 Cor. 5:17*), or again, "for in Christ Jesus you are all children of God through faith" (*Gal. 3:26*). For each of us to be "in Christ" is for each of us to be joined to all others who are "in Christ," so that my Lord and Savior is always our Lord and Savior. Thus, while each of us affirms gladly that Jesus Christ is "my (personal) Lord and Savior," we cannot claim that Jesus Christ is "my (private) Lord and Savior."

English translations of the New Testament reinforce tendencies toward individualistic faith. The English word *you* can mean either *you* (singular) or *you* (plural), referring to one person or a group of people. New Testament Greek, like most languages, has separate words for second person singular and plural pronouns: *su* is you (singular) while *humeis* is you (plural). When we encounter Jesus saying, "You are the salt of the earth," we may miss his meaning: "Humeis are the salt of the earth—You all, together, are the salt of the earth." When Jesus said, "If you keep my commandments, you

iBelieve

will abide in my love" (*John 15:10*), he was not addressing individuals, but the community: "If you all, together, keep my commandments, you all, together, will abide in my love." Again, Paul's well-known encouragement—"I am confident . . . that the one who began a good work among you will bring it to completion by the day of Jesus Christ" (*Phil. 1:6*)—was addressed to the community: " . . . the one who began a good work among you all, together . . . ."

None of this is to say that the gospel is impersonal, that the individual is lost in a faceless mass. The gospel is truly personal because it places us in relationships with other persons. The person whose Lord and Savior is Jesus Christ is saved from the isolation of individualism and is placed within God's new Way of fully personal relationships in a community of mutual love. Jesus Christ is my Lord and Savior, but my salvation and my life in God's new Way are not separate from the relationships of family, friends, cities, nations, the world. My Lord and Savior Jesus Christ is always our Lord and Savior Jesus Christ.

Do you not know that all of us who have been baptized into Christ Jesus were baptized into his death? Therefore we have been buried with him by Baptism into death, so that, just as Christ was raised from the dead by the glory of the Father, so we too might walk in newness of life.

—Romans 6:3–4

"Who is your Lord and Savior?" Baptism is a profound instance of the truly personal nature of Christian faith and life. In Baptism, all the promises of God are focused on one human life; the entire "history of salvation" culminates in the words "You are baptized in the name of the Father, and of the Son, and of the Holy Spirit." Yet Baptism is not a private moment, for the whole community of baptized persons gathers to bear witness to the grace of the Lord Jesus Christ, the love of God, and the communion of the Holy Spirit. The church—in this place, and in all times and places—confesses common faith and welcomes each person into common life.

"Do you not know that all of us who have been baptized into Christ Jesus were baptized into his death?" asks Paul (*Rom. 6:3*). In Baptism we are all joined to Christ, "buried with him by Baptism into death." But death never has the final word. United with Jesus Christ in his death, we are certainly united with him in resurrection, for " . . . just as Christ was raised from the dead by the glory of the Father, so we too might walk in newness of life" (*Rom. 6:4*). The "newness" of Baptismal life takes shape in a new community of all the baptized, for as we are united to Jesus Christ in his death and resurrection, we become the body of Christ: "so we, who are many, are one body in Christ, and individually we are members one of another" (*Rom. 12:5*).

Baptism places us in a new being-saved community of women and men who are united to Christ and therefore joined to one another. The characteristic act of this new body of Christ is Eucharist—thanksgiving—and the characteristic expression of thanksgiving is the Eucharist—the Lord's Supper. "The cup of blessing that we bless, is it not a sharing in the blood of Christ?" asks Paul. "The bread that we break, is it not a sharing in the body

iBelieve

of Christ?" (*1 Cor. 10:16*) In the sharing of the bread and wine, we are joined to Jesus Christ in his death and resurrection. In the sharing of bread and wine, we are joined to one another: "Because there is one bread, we who are many are one body, for we all partake of the one bread" (*1 Cor. 10:17*). As the gathered community shares bread and wine, it shares new life in Christ.

Day 34 | The Church's Sacraments

And Jesus came and said to them, "All authority in heaven and on earth has been given to me. Go therefore and make disciples of all nations, baptizing them in the name of the Father and of the Son and of the Holy Spirit, and teaching them to obey everything that I have commanded you. And remember, I am with you always, to the end of the age."
—Matthew 28:18–20

Baptism and Eucharist—the church's Sacraments—are profoundly personal events precisely because they are profoundly communal events. Becoming ". . . alive to God in Christ Jesus" (*Rom. 6:11*), we become alive to one another in Christ Jesus. We, together, are the body of Christ. But there is more. Baptism and Eucharist are expressions of God's grace for the community of faith, the church. Yet the grace of the Lord Jesus Christ, the love of God, and the communion of the Holy Spirit are never the church's possessions. "All this is from God, who reconciled us to himself through Christ" (*2 Cor. 5:18*).

In Baptism we know the gracious love of God in Christ. God does not love us and become one with us and abide with us because we have earned God's favor. God's love is gracious, free movement among us, joining us to Jesus Christ and to one another. As baptized people, we are called to live out God's grace in a common life of service to all people. We cannot, then, require that others deserve our loving service before we will give it. The church's God-given "ministry of reconciliation" is its free service to a wounded, fractured world.

In the Eucharist we know the self-giving love of God in Jesus Christ. As we share the bread and wine, we are beckoned outside the upper room in order that we, too, may feed the thousands and that we, too, may eat and drink with "sinners." God shares God's very self with us in Jesus Christ. In thankful response, we share God's gifts with one another in the Lord's Supper. Eucharist then beckons us to share who we are and what we have with a world in desperate need. As John says, "How does God's love abide in anyone who has the world's goods and sees a brother or sister in need and yet refuses help?" (*1 John 3:17*)

Baptism, Eucharist, and Ministry

All this is from God, who reconciled us to himself through Christ, and has given us the ministry of reconciliation; that is, in Christ God was reconciling the world to himself, not counting their trespasses against them, and entrusting the message of reconciliation to us.
—*2 Corinthians 5:18–19*

Our ministry of reconciliation is not a grinding duty, but the living out of our salvation as we follow our Lord in God's Way. Being alive to God in Christ Jesus is not restricted to private life or limited to church life; it embraces all of life. New life in Christ is not confined to personal fulfillment or congregational enhancement, for it reaches out to embrace the whole of God's world. Ministry is not an obligation imposed on Christians or on the Christian community; it is the very shape of new life in God's Way.

Christian preaching and teaching sometimes separates theology and ethics, faith and life. We are sometimes told that the first order of Christian business is to believe correctly, and that "good works" are secondary to faith. The reality of the gospel is different, however. We believe that God's grace in Jesus Christ has placed us within a new Way of living. Our faith is more than intellectual assent to a series of theological propositions. Our faith is trusting participation in God's salvation; faith and life are one. James, in his characteristically gruff way, says, "[F]aith by itself, if it has no works, is dead" (*James 2:17*). It would not be misrepresenting James to say that faith, if it has no works, is not faith at all.

Baptism, Eucharist, and ministry are parts of a whole; grace, gratitude, and service are three aspects of one new life in Christ. Baptism without Eucharist is nothing more than a cute, cultural rite for cuddly babies. Baptism and Eucharist without ministry are only smug expressions of churchly narcissism. Ministry without Baptism and Eucharist is a futile exercise in self-sufficiency. Being alive to God in Jesus Christ is living the whole of life in fidelity to God's new Way in the world, together with Jesus Christ, who is "the pioneer and perfecter of our faith" (*Heb. 12:2*).

NOTES:

Further Thoughts

Day 36 Romans 6:1–11; Psalm 114

What then are we to say? Should we continue in sin in order that grace may abound? By no means! How can we who died to sin go on living in it? Do you not know that all of us who have been baptized into Christ Jesus were baptized into his death? Therefore we have been buried with him by Baptism into death, so that, just as Christ was raised from the dead by the glory of the Father, so we too might walk in newness of life. For if we have been united with him in a death like his, we will certainly be united with him in a resurrection like his. We know that our old self was crucified with him so that the body of sin might be destroyed, and we might no longer be enslaved to sin. For whoever has died is freed from sin. But if we have died with Christ, we believe that we will also live with him. We know that Christ, being raised from the dead, will never die again; death no longer has dominion over him. The death he died, he died to sin, once for all; but the life he lives, he lives to God. So you also must consider yourselves dead to sin and alive to God in Christ Jesus.

—Romans 6:1–11

When Israel went out from Egypt,
the house of Jacob from a people of strange language,
Judah became God's sanctuary, Israel his dominion.
The sea looked and fled; Jordan turned back.
The mountains skipped like rams, the hills like lambs.
Why is it, O sea, that you flee? O Jordan, that you turn back?
O mountains, that you skip like rams? O hills, like lambs?
Tremble, O earth, at the presence of the Lord,
at the presence of the God of Jacob,
who turns the rock into a pool of water,
the flint into a spring of water.

—Psalm 114

iBelieve

Crucified, Dead, and Buried

Then he began to teach them that the Son of Man must undergo great suffering, and be rejected by the elders, the chief priests, and the scribes, and be killed, and after three days rise again. He said all this quite openly. And Peter took him aside and began to rebuke him. But turning and looking at his disciples, he rebuked Peter and said, "Get behind me, Satan! For you are setting your mind not on divine things but on human things."
—Mark 8:31–33

The Gospels are not "lives of Jesus." We might even say that they are "deaths of Jesus." Each of the Gospels narrates the events of Jesus' crucifixion in excruciating detail, for that event is the defining angle of vision on his life. We know about Jesus' words and deeds just what the Gospel writers knew: what he said and did got him killed! This simple fact is indispensable for understanding Jesus. Was Jesus a caring healer who moved with compassion among the sick and disabled? Well, yes, but if that was all he was, why was he executed for it? Was Jesus a wise teacher whose sayings pointed the way to a fulfilling life? Again, yes, but if he was only that, why were people so outraged that they crucified him? Was Jesus a good man who served the needs of the less fortunate? Of course, but if that is all there is, why was he killed?

Jesus' opponents understood him well. They knew that the Way of God proclaimed by Jesus turned "the way things are" upside down, requiring a radical reorientation of life. When Jesus proclaimed, "The Kingdom of God has come near," he did not continue, "Isn't that a delightful possibility to make your life happier and more fulfilling?" Jesus said, "Repent!" Jesus calls us to stop dead in our tracks, turn around from the way we are going, and trust in the dramatically new Way of God. Jesus is not a confirmation of all our aspirations, but the one whose words and actions proclaim something radically new. God with us calls for a denial of "the way things are" with us, and a turning toward the Way of God.

73

Day 38 Right Belief, Faithful Living

We must no longer be children, tossed to and fro and blown about by every wind of doctrine, by people's trickery, by their craftiness in deceitful scheming. But speaking the truth in love, we must grow up in every way into him who is the head, into Christ, from whom the whole body, joined and knit together by every ligament with which it is equipped, as each part is working properly, promotes the body's growth in building itself up in love.

—Ephesians 4:14–16

Ordinary people often become impatient with theological discussion that becomes abstract and far removed from everyday realities. "Simple faith" and "theology" are not alien to one another, however. The capacity to articulate faith clearly and convincingly is crucial to faith itself. If Christians do not understand the central affirmations of their faith, the church's proclamation will be weakened and faith itself may be diminished.

When we read the New Testament, we encounter the earliest Christian expressions of the meaning of the good news of Jesus Christ. The Gospels are not mere biographies of Jesus, and the letters are more than chatty exchanges. John's Gospel was written "so that you may come to believe that Jesus is the Messiah [the Christ], the Son of God, and that through believing you may have life in his name" (*John 20:31*). The necessity of right belief is clear in Paul's warning to the Galatians that "there are some who are confusing you and want to pervert the gospel of Christ" (*Gal. 1:7*). The earliest church understood that there is an integral relationship between right belief and faithful living. (See *Eph. 4:14, 15.*)

Throughout its history, the Christian community's concern for right belief has been far more than a fascination with intellectual orthodoxy. What we believe to be true affects how we live. What we believe about "Jesus Christ, Lord and Savior" makes a difference in how we understand God's Way in the world, and how we live our way in the world.

Freedom from the Power of Sin and Death

> *I consider that the sufferings of this present time are not worth comparing with the glory about to be revealed to us. For the creation waits with eager longing for the revealing of the children of God; for the creation was subjected to futility, not of its own will but by the will of the one who subjected it, in hope that the creation itself will be set free from its bondage to decay and will obtain the freedom of the glory of the children of God. We know that the whole creation has been groaning in labor pains until now; and not only the creation, but we ourselves, who have the first fruits of the Spirit, groan inwardly while we wait for adoption, the redemption of our bodies. For in hope we were saved. Now hope that is seen is not hope. For who hopes for what is seen? But if we hope for what we do not see, we wait for it with patience.*
> —Romans 8:18–25

Salvation in Jesus Christ is nothing less than freedom from the power of sin and death. "So if anyone is in Christ," says Paul, "there is a new creation: everything old has passed away; see, everything has become new!" (*2 Cor. 5:17*). We are no longer captive to sin's power to separate us from God; we are no longer imprisoned by the finality of death. In Christ, God has created new life for the world, overcoming the necessity of human alienation from God, enmity among people, and estrangement between human beings and the rest of God's good creation. Through the life, death, and resurrection of Jesus Christ, creation is freed from its "bondage to decay," liberated for "the freedom of the glory of the children of God" (*Rom. 8:21*).

Salvation is not limited to new life beyond death, although salvation encompasses our eternal life with God. Salvation is a present reality in this life as well as the certain hope of life to come. God's Way in this world can be our way, unchained from the burden of sin and guilt. That is why the good news of salvation is expressed so often in acclamations of God's new creation of human life in Christ.

Day 40 | Alive with Christ

For it is in Christ that the complete being of the Godhead dwells embodied, and in him you have been brought to completion. Every power and authority in the universe is subject to him as Head. . . . For in Baptism you were buried with him, in Baptism also you were raised to life with him through your faith in the active power of God who raised him from the dead. And although you were dead because of your sins . . . he has made you alive with Christ.

—*Colossians 2:9–13, NEB*

The truth of the gospel is far more than a system of doctrine to which Christians must adhere. The truth is that the gospel is good news for men and women who, in Christ, can live new lives within God's Way, free from captivity to "the way things are." Liberated by our Savior Jesus Christ, we find ourselves in a community whose Lord is the same Jesus Christ. The Lord Jesus Christ leads this community of faith in the Way of God, a Way that leads us beyond ourselves in the whole of creation.

We are "alive with Christ" (*Col 2:13*, NEB) and "alive to God in Christ Jesus" (Rom. 6:11). Our faith, then, is the expression of our living relationship with the One who created, redeems, and sustains the cosmos. God is not an incomprehensible deity, concealed in inaccessible mystery. We are not reduced to vague speculation about the meaning and purpose of life. We do not have to guess about the way we are to live. Because God has drawn near to us in the life, death, and resurrection of Jesus Christ, we can draw near to God. The letter to the Hebrews invites us to "hold fast to our confession," and to "approach the throne of grace with boldness, so that we may receive mercy and find grace to help in time of need" (*Heb. 4:14, 16*). Our confession is that "Jesus Christ is my Lord and Savior." Because Jesus Christ is Lord and Savior of each of us and of all of us together, we are truly alive—to God, to each other, and to the world!

I Believe:
40 Daily Readings
for the Purposeful Presbyterian

Alive to God in Jesus Christ

SMALL-GROUP STUDY GUIDE
By Mark D. Hinds

Introduction

This study guide is designed to aid group study by providing five session plans for use during your reading of *I Believe: 40 Daily Readings for the Purposeful Presbyterian*. These session plans include a variety of educational methods; the leader of the group study will have the responsibility of choosing the methods that are most appropriate to your group. Each participant in the study should have a copy of this book and should make a commitment to participating in each session. As you prepare to lead the group study, you will want to:

- Read the daily entries.

- Skim through this study guide, noting any activity that will require advance preparation.

- Obtain teaching and learning resources recommended in the session plans, such as newsprint and markers, masking tape, *The Presbyterian Hymnal*, the *Book of Common Worship*, paper, and pencils.

- Focus on the main idea.

- Prepare the meeting space, based on your leadership style. For example, a circle of chairs is conducive to a leader who seeks to foster an open discussion; chairs around a table offer a good space for writing and discussion; and a lectern facing a block of chairs works best for a lecture presentation.

- Pray for the Holy Spirit's guidance.

Coordinating Daily Devotionals and Study Sessions

It will be important for the participants to be on the same page, as it were. Consider calling the group together for an orientation to the study at least one week before the first session. During this orientation session, distribute copies of the book to the participants. Prepare a reading schedule for distribution to the group; for example, if your group meets on Sundays:

Sunday, (*insert date here*): Read Day 1

Monday, (*insert date here*): Read Day 2

Tuesday, (*insert date here*): Read Day 3

Wednesday, (*insert date here*): Read Day 4

Thursday, (*insert date here*): Read Day 5

Friday, (*insert date here*): Read Day 6

Saturday, (*insert date here*): Read Day 7

Sunday, (*insert date here*): Study Session 1; Read Day 8 . . . etc.

Also note for the group that five additional daily readings (Days 36–40) follow Session 5. You may agree as a group to meet a final time after Day 40 to evaluate the book and the study sessions. This could also be a time of worship and celebration for your group.

For future study options, please visit www.pcusa.org/witherspoon for additional titles in the *I Believe* series.

SMALL-GROUP STUDY
For discussion of Days 1–7 in the daily reader;
to be used after Day 7

Session 1

"JESUS Christ Is My Lord and Savior"

MAIN IDEA

The name Jesus conveys his primary identity and calling: Beloved of God and Savior.

PREPARING TO LEAD

- Read the articles for Days 1–7.

- Read through this session and choose activities and discussion topics. Be open to asking questions that arise from your reading of the book.

- Place a glass bowl with water in the center of the group's meeting space. Place small, smooth stones in the bowl, enough for every group member to have one.

- Reflect on your Baptism, what it means to you, what comfort it brings. This session will focus on the importance of naming in the service of Baptism. What does your name mean? Who named you and why? Reflect on the belief that God names the baptized beloved children.

Option: If your group has access to a TV and DVD player, consider showing a video clip of a Baptism. Baptisms are shown in *O Brother, Where Art Thou?*, *My Big Fat Greek Wedding*, and *The Apostle*. Following the video clip, invite group members to reflect on the ways in which Baptism is portrayed.

GATHERING ACTIVITIES

- Welcome. As group members arrive, extend words and gestures of welcome. Consider providing name tags and pens. Give some thought to asking another group member to provide refreshments.

- Opening worship. After a brief time of informal conversation, invite the group members to gather around the bowl filled with water and stones. Read the following words from the Baptism liturgy:

> In the waters of Jordan
> Jesus was baptized by John
> and anointed with your Spirit.
> By the Baptism of his own death and resurrection,
> Christ set us free from sin and death,
> and opened the way to eternal life.
> We thank you, O God, for the water of Baptism.
> In it we are buried with Christ in his death.
> From it we are raised to share in his resurrection.
> Through it we are reborn by the power of the Holy Spirit.[1]

Pass the bowl of water to the first person, inviting him or her to dip fingers in the water and to remove a stone, as you say his or her name and the words "Remember your Baptism and be thankful." That person then passes the bowl to the next, saying that person's name and repeating the words. Continue until each person has received the bowl and removed a stone. Suggest to the group that the stones are "stones of remembrance." Ask the group to carry their stones throughout the duration of the study as a way to remember their Baptisms and to be thankful.

Option: Provide waterproof markers and invite group members to write their names on the stones.

GUIDING THE DISCUSSION

- Exploring Baptism

  ☒ Invite group members to share stories about how they came to be named. What significance do their names hold for them? How have their names helped shape their identities?

1. *Book of Common Worship* (Louisville: Westminster/John Knox Press, 1993), 439. Used by permission.

iBelieve

☑ How did the group members feel during the gathering worship, specifically when they heard their names called in reference to Baptism? Invite the group to share stories of their Baptisms. How have their Baptisms helped shape their identities?

☑ One of the most significant aspects of the service of Baptism is that the one being baptized is named. Read the following statements aloud and invite group members' comments:

The elder announces the name of the candidate as part of the presentation. The use of a person's name in Baptism is its most important use in all of the Christian liturgy, for it marks adoption into the family of God. One's name is an extension of one's identity, a sign of one's uniqueness as a human being.[2]

In the act of Baptism, the minister addresses the candidate, using only the candidate's Christian (given) name(s). . . . In Baptism, we are reborn into a new family, the family of the triune God. Baptized, we are made sisters and brothers together in a family that transcends the family of our physical birth. In a sense, we are given a new surname: the name Christian. Thus the minister uses only the candidate's Christian (given) name.[3]

- Exploring Scripture

☑ Invite the group to recall Bible stories that feature names and naming. They might remember Jacob wrestling the stranger, after which he receives the name Israel (*Gen. 32*); Simon's confession of Jesus as the

2. *Companion to the Book of Common Worship,* Peter Bower, ed. (Louisville: Geneva Press, 2003), 159.
3. *Companion to the Book of Common Worship,* Peter Bower, ed. (Louisville: Geneva Press, 2003), 159.

Messiah and his new name, Peter (*Matt. 16*); and Saul becoming Paul (*Acts 9*). What is the significance of naming in these stories?

☞ Read Mark 1:9–11. Invite volunteers to portray John, Jesus, the voice and the narrator in a dramatic reading of the text. Following the reading, ask the group: What does the voice from heaven name Jesus? What does this mean for all who are baptized? (This is a promise for all who are baptized, that God names us beloved children.)

- Exploring the Daily Readings

  ☑ In the reading for Day 2, the author conveys the rich significance of the names Mary and Jesus for Israel. Invite group members to summarize the significance of these names and what they say about Mary and Jesus' role in the Gospel story.

  ☑ Read the paragraph on Day 5 that begins "As with Jesus' words and deeds, his death and resurrection demand a response and require a decision." Ask the group to talk about decisions they have made in response to Jesus Christ.

  ☑ Read the statement on Day 7 that begins "We are Christians if . . . ." Ask the group members if they agree or disagree with this statement. If this statement is true, what implications does it hold for people who name Jesus Christ Lord and Savior?

Concluding the Session

- Singing our faith. Lead the group in reading the text of the hymn "Baptized in Water," no. 492 in *The Presbyterian Hymnal*. Ask group members to call out words and phrases in the text that express the way they feel about their Baptisms. After a brief time of sharing, sing the hymn together.

iBelieve

- Conclude with a prayer, asking God to use the stones of remembrance to remind the group members that they are beloved children of God.

NOTES:

SMALL-GROUP STUDY
For discussion of Days 8–14 in the daily reader;
to be used after Day 14

*S*ession 2

"Jesus CHRIST Is My Lord and Savior"

MAIN IDEA
To name Jesus "Christ" is to make a startling affirmation of faith.

PREPARING TO LEAD
- Read the daily reader, Days 8–14.

- Read through this session and choose activities and discussion topics. Be open to asking questions that arise from your reading of the book.

- Place a glass bowl with water in the center of the group's meeting space. Place small, smooth stones in the bowl, enough for each new member of the group to have one.

- Reflect on the commitment to Jesus Christ that Baptism entails. Describe a Christ-like way of life that being baptized calls you to pursue.

GATHERING ACTIVITIES
- Welcome. As group members arrive, extend words and gestures of welcome. Consider providing name tags and pens. Give some thought to asking another group member to provide refreshments.

- Opening worship. After a brief time of informal conversation, invite the group members to gather around the bowl filled with water and stones. Pass the bowl of water to group members, inviting them to touch the water and, if they were not present during the last session, to remove a stone. Invite the group to touch their wet fingers to their foreheads and say, "I am baptized." Offer a prayer of thanks to God for sending Christ to save, guide, and protect God's beloved children.

GUIDING THE DISCUSSION

- Exploring Baptism

  > The "remembrance stones" are a good way to keep the promise and challenge of our Baptisms before us. Invite the group members to share stories from the past week that relate to remembering their Baptisms. Ask: Did carrying the stone aid you in remembering and provide comfort in a particular situation? Did the memory of being God's beloved child provide strength for a particularly difficult day?

  > The Baptism liturgy tells us that Baptism is both a gift and a responsibility. God claims us through the act; we claim God by living lives of grateful obedience to Jesus Christ. Read the following excerpt aloud and invite comments from the group:

  > The Christian life involves both a *turning from* sin and bondage to evil and a *turning to* Christ and the way of righteousness. It is to turn our backs on the kind of life that is destructive and to embrace the new life that is promised in the Gospel. Both renunciation and affirmation . . . are equally dependent on God's grace active in our lives and in the community of faith. . . .

  > In the ancient church, this [turning from and turning toward] was expressed in a dramatic way. Immediately before Baptism, candidates were asked to face west and renounce evil. The west, as the place of the setting sun and gathering darkness, symbolized the abode of evil. The candidates then *turned from* the west and *turned to* the east and professed the Christian faith. . . . [T]hose early Christians literally turned their backs on the ways of Satan and his darkness as they faced the altar and affirmed the ways of Christ.[1]

1. *Companion to the Book of Common Worship,* Peter Bower, ed. (Louisville: Geneva Press, 2003), 159–60.

88

☑ What other symbolic acts could help us remember the "turning from, turning toward" that is central to the Christian way of life? What symbolic act could be performed with the remembrance stones that might help us remember the significant commitment Baptism entails?

- Exploring Scripture

    ☒ Turn to the Old Testament and look up several references to the expected Messiah: Isaiah 9:6–7; 11:1–9; 49:6–7; 55:1–5; Daniel 7:13–14; Zephaniah 3:14–20; Malachi 3:1–5; 4:1–6. As a group, compile a list of Israel's expectations of the Messiah.

    ☒ Ask the group to read Philippians 2:5–11 and determine to what extent Jesus met expectations of the Messiah as reflected in the Old Testament readings. In what ways did Jesus confound the Old Testament's expectations of Messiah?

    ☒ Compare the verbs used in the second article of The Apostles' Creed with those used in Philippians 2:5–11. *print Apostles' creed* What do these verbs tell you about the work of Jesus Christ? Are the verbs mostly active or passive?

- Exploring the Daily Readings

    ☑ Ask: How do you understand the author's statement "'Christ' is not a name, of course; it is a confession of faith" (Day 9)?

    ☒ On Day 10, the author writes: "The 'Christ hymn' in Philippians 2:6–11 is a bold proclamation of the unified reality. The hymn expresses eloquently the significance of the life, death, and resurrection of Jesus the Christ. He was one with us, even to the point of death. Because of his absolute identification with human life, God raised him from the dead. The crucified Jesus is the risen Christ; the risen Christ is the crucified Jesus.

One makes no Christian sense apart from the other." Invite the group to comment on the statement. Do they agree with it? If not, why not?

CONCLUDING THE SESSION

To close, call the group to reaffirm their Baptisms by standing and answering the following questions (suggest that they stand facing the west and turn toward the east after the first question):

Leader: Through Baptism we enter the covenant God has established. Within this covenant God gives us new life, guards us from evil, and nurtures us in love. In embracing that covenant, we choose whom we will serve, by turning from evil and turning to Jesus Christ. Trusting in the gracious mercy of God, do you turn from the ways of sin and renounce evil and its power in the world?
People: I do.
Leader: Who is your Lord and Savior?
People: Jesus Christ is my Lord and Savior.
Leader: Will you be Christ's faithful disciple, obeying his Word and showing his love?
People: I will, with God's help.

- Sing or read in unison "At the Name of Jesus," no. 148 in *The Presbyterian Hymnal*, as a closing prayer.

NOTES:

SMALL-GROUP STUDY
For discussion of Days 15–21 in the daily reader;
to be used after Day 21

$\mathcal{S}$ession **3**

"Jesus Christ Is My LORD and Savior"

MAIN IDEA

Jesus Christ is Lord, not according to the way the world defines "lordship," but as God redefines it. Baptism is both tomb (death to the old life) and womb (raised to the new life).

PREPARING TO LEAD

- Read the daily reader, Days 15–21.

- Read through this session and choose activities and discussion topics. Be open to asking questions that arise from your reading of the book.

- Place a glass bowl with water in the center of the group's meeting space. Place small, smooth stones in the bowl, enough for each new member of the group to have one.

- Reflect on the author's contention that the crucifixion redefines "lordship" and "power." What does it mean to you to personally confess a Lord who exercises power through the cross?

GATHERING ACTIVITIES

- Welcome. As group members arrive, extend words and gestures of welcome. Consider providing name tags and pens. Give some thought to asking another group member to provide refreshments.

- Opening worship. After a brief time of informal conversation, invite the group members to gather around the bowl filled with water and stones. As in the previous session, pass the bowl of water to group members, inviting them to touch the water. Also invite each new member to remove a stone. Invite the group to touch their wet fingers to their foreheads and say, "I am baptized." Offer a prayer of thanks to God for sending Christ to save, guide, and protect God's beloved children.

Invite group members to share stories of how their stones of remembrance helped them remember their Baptisms during the previous week.

GUIDING THE DISCUSSION

- Exploring Baptism

   Read the following excerpt:

  > Water is basic to life. Before each of us was born, water protected us in our mother's womb. We cleanse our bodies with it. It brings cooling refreshment. It sustains life on our planet. Without water we will die. But by it we may die, for water also has power to kill. We can drown in it. Floods destroy life and property. This is why water speaks so forcefully in Baptism when used in abundance. The power of the symbolism of water is particularly dramatic where a Baptismal pool or font is kept full of flowing water. Throughout history, the place of Baptism has been regarded as a bath by which we are cleansed of sin, a womb from which we are reborn, a tomb in which we are buried with Christ and from which we are raised with him. This is more readily apparent when the Baptismal space is ample and the Baptismal font or pool is prominently located.[1]

  Ask: Of the three—bath, womb, and tomb—which seems the most powerful symbol for Baptism? Why? Which is the most startling?

- Exploring Scripture

  Read the following passages that reference Baptism: Romans 6:1–11, Galatians 3:25–28. Ask the group to decide which images are suggested by the passages:

1. *Companion to the Book of Common Worship,* Peter Bower, ed. (Louisville: Geneva Press, 2003), 161.

womb and/or tomb? (What does Galatians mean by being clothed in Christ?)

- Study the "young man" in Mark 14:51–52 and 16:5. Note that an unnamed young man runs away and out of his clothes at Jesus' arrest. Is this the same young man that appears in the empty tomb in 16:5? Now he is described as "dressed in a white robe." (Clothed in Christ?) Some have suggested that the presence of this young man frames the crucifixion, death, burial, and resurrection of Jesus. In the ancient church, converts were baptized in the nude and given a white robe, to signify Romans 6:3–5. Invite the group to wonder together what if any association with Baptism the presence of this young man suggests.

- Exploring the Daily Readings

  - A key question in the Baptism service is "Who is your Lord and Savior?" How does your answer to the question "Who is your Lord?" shape your identity and your calling in life?

  - On Day 18, the author writes: "The cross turns all human standards inside out, revealing the impossible possibility that '. . . God's foolishness is wiser than human wisdom, and God's weakness is stronger than human strength' " (1 Cor. 1:25). If Jesus Christ is Lord, then our notions of power and authority—both God's and our own—must undergo transformation by being conformed to the gospel." What are your notions of power and authority? How does the cross redefine your notions? How does that affect the way you live your life?

  - Distribute copies of the Barmen Declaration (Book of Confessions, PC(USA), 8.01–.28). How does Barmen define lordship? What specific phrases were dangerous to confess in Nazi Germany? What specific phrases could be dangerous to confess in twenty-first-century America? What difficult stances does your Baptism into Christ call you to take?

Concluding the Session

- Sing or read in unison "We Know That Christ Is Raised," no. 495 in *The Presbyterian Hymnal.* Conclude with a time for the participants to reflect on what it means for them to call Jesus Christ "Lord." Invite a member of the group to pray. Remind each person, "You are baptized."

Notes:

SMALL-GROUP STUDY
For discussion of Days 22–28 in the daily reader;
to be used after Day 28

"Jesus Christ Is My Lord and SAVIOR"

MAIN IDEA
Jesus Christ is Lord and SAVIOR.

PREPARING TO LEAD
- Read the daily reader, Days 22–28.
- Read through this session and choose activities and discussion topics. Be open to asking questions that arise from your reading of the book.
- Place a glass bowl with water in the center of the group's meeting space. Place small, smooth stones in the bowl, enough for each new member of the group to have one.

GATHERING ACTIVITIES
- Welcome. As group members arrive, extend words and gestures of welcome. Consider providing name tags and pens. Give some thought to asking another group member to provide refreshments.
- Opening worship. After a brief time of informal conversation, invite the group members to gather around the bowl filled with water and stones. Offer the following prayer:

  Send your Spirit to move over this water
  that it may be a fountain of deliverance and rebirth.
  Wash away the *sin* of all who *are* cleansed by it.
  Raise them to new life,
  and graft *them* to the body of Christ.
  Pour out your Holy Spirit upon *them*,
  that *they* may have power to do your will,
  and continue forever in the risen life of Christ.
  To you, Father, Son, and Holy Spirit, one God,
  be all praise, honor, and glory,
  now and forever.
  Amen.[1]

1. *Book of Common Worship* (Louisville: Westminster/John Knox Press, 1993), 411. Used by permission.

As in the previous session, pass the bowl of water to group members, inviting them to touch the water. Also invite each new member to remove a stone. Invite the group to touch their wet fingers to their foreheads and say, "Wash me and I will be clean."

Invite group members to share stories of how their stones of remembrance helped them remember their Baptisms during the previous week.

GUIDING THE DISCUSSION

* Exploring Baptism

☑ Read the following excerpt:

The washing with water in the name of the triune God is at the heart of the Sacrament [of Baptism], both theologically and dramatically. In the early centuries, Baptism was usually by immersion. However, this need not have meant full submersion in the water. Early Christian mosaics portray persons kneeling or standing in the Baptismal pool as water is poured over them (that is, affusion). Whatever the practice, Baptism connoted *going down* into the water (dying) and *coming up* out of the water (rising). In later centuries, when the Baptism of adults was rare, fonts were still large enough to immerse infants. Eastern Orthodox churches continue to immerse infants to the present day. While the quantity of water applied in Baptism does not affect the validity of the Sacrament, lavish actions are best for enacting this Sacrament of lavish grace. As the rubric indicates, water should be used "visibly and generously."[2]

☐ Invite the group to share their observations and feelings about Baptism as a cleansing based on this excerpt.

2. *Companion to the Book of Common Worship,* Peter Bower, ed. (Louisville: Geneva Press, 2003), 162–63.

iBelieve

☐ Last session, we considered Baptism through the metaphors "tomb" and "womb"; we who are baptized die with Christ and are reborn to new life. This session, we look at Baptism through the image of "bathing": all who are baptized are cleansed from sin. Ask: What is sin?

- Exploring Scripture

  ☐ In the book of Judges, it is said that the tribe of Benjamin's army contained an elite group of seven hundred left-handers who could "sling a stone at a hair, and not miss" (20:16). According to the original Hebrew wording, they could throw at a hair and not "sin." Both the Hebrew and Greek words for "sin" mean "to miss." Discuss with the group their experiences of sin as "missing the mark."

  ☐ Read Psalm 51:1–17. Invite the group to reflect on the tone and message of the psalm as a prayer of confession. Could this psalm serve as a corporate prayer of confession during your church's worship service? Why or why not?

  ☐ In Romans 7:14–25, Paul struggles with the problem of sin. Can you say with Paul, "For I know that nothing good dwells within me, that is, in my flesh"? (v. 18a). Why or why not? In Paul's thought, what is the answer to the power of sin? (Read into Romans 8.)

- Exploring the Daily Readings.

  ☐ A key question in the Baptism service is "Who is your Lord and Savior?" How does your answer to the question "Who is your Savior?" shape your identity and your calling in life? From what are we saved?

  ☐ From Day 26: "We misunderstand the reality of sin if we imagine checklists that catalog good and bad deeds, right and wrong actions. Sin is far more than the debit

iBelieve

column on a moral balance sheet. Sin is nothing less than a powerful force that turns us away from God's Way, bending us toward easy acceptance of 'the way things are.' "

Ask: How have you experienced sin as "a powerful force that turns [you] away from God's Way?"

 From Day 28: "We need a Savior, One who can set us free from constant striving and from constant failure to achieve full communion with God and with other people." What is "full communion with God"? With others?

CONCLUDING THE SESSION

• Sing or read in unison "Have Mercy On Us, Living Lord," no. 195 in *The Presbyterian Hymnal.* Conclude with a time for the participants to reflect on what it means for them to call Jesus Christ "Savior." Invite a member of the group to pray. Remind each person, "You are baptized."

NOTES:

Judy-
Ken Bartlett-
Lewis- cousisns death *Rocky's*
Scott Covington-
Lilian-
Fred clark-

SMALL-GROUP STUDY
For discussion of Days 29–35 in the daily reader;
to be used after Day 35

*S*ession
5

"Jesus Christ IS MY Lord and Savior"

MAIN IDEA

God has no grandchildren. In Christ, we are all children of God.

PREPARING TO LEAD

- Read the daily reader, Days 29–35.

- Read through this session and choose activities and discussion topics. Be open to asking questions that arise from your reading of the book.

- Place a glass bowl with water in the center of the group's meeting space.

GATHERING ACTIVITIES

- Welcome. As group members arrive, extend words and gestures of welcome. Consider providing name tags and pens. Give some thought to asking another group member to provide refreshments.

- Opening worship. After a brief time of informal conversation, invite the group members to gather around the bowl filled with water. As in the previous session, pass the bowl of water to group members, inviting them to touch the water. Invite the group to touch their wet fingers to their foreheads and say, "I am baptized."

  Option: Invite group members to touch the water and make the sign of the cross on the forehead of another participant, saying, "Remember your Baptism and be thankful." (Clarify with the group that this is *not* Baptism, but another way to celebrate its remembrance.)

  Invite group members to share stories of how their stones of remembrance helped them remember their Baptisms during the previous week.

GUIDING THE DISCUSSION

- Exploring Baptism

     Read the following excerpt:

    It is highly appropriate to follow Baptism with a celebration of the Lord's Supper. When the two sacraments are celebrated in the same service, their intimate relationship is emphasized. God creates the church through Baptism and sustains the church with the Supper. From ancient times, Christian initiation culminated with the new Christians joining the congregation at the Holy Table.[1]

    Ask: Have you ever attended a worship service in which both Baptism and Communion were celebrated? Share observations and feelings about it. Was an explicit connection made between the two sacraments?

    Discuss this statement: Every Christian worship service necessarily includes both Baptism and Eucharist. Without both sacraments, worship is not Christian.

- Exploring Scripture

    Romans 6:1–11 has provided much of the scriptural warrant for this study. Take some time to read that passage in the Bible slowly and meditatively. Invite the group members to share their thoughts and feelings when they hear/read this passage.

    Galatians 3:23–28 is one of Paul's most central teachings on Baptism. Focus on the metaphor of being "clothed in Christ." The clothing metaphor could relate to the Baptismal practice of dressing the newly baptized in a white robe. What else could "clothed in Christ" mean?

---

1. *Companion to the Book of Common Worship,* Peter Bower, ed. (Louisville: Geneva Press, 2003), 166.

- ☑ Those who are "in Christ" belong to God. Ask the group to think of favorite biblical passages that reassure them that they do belong to God.
- Exploring the Daily Readings
    - ☑ From Day 32: Describe the difference between being "in Christ" and "Christ in me."
    - ☑ From Day 33: "As the gathered community shares bread and wine it shares new life in Christ."

        List other specific, concrete ways in which the community of faith shares new life together. What is meant by "new" in the phrase "new life in Christ"?
    - ☑ From Day 35: "Baptism without Eucharist is nothing more than a cute, cultural rite for cuddly babies. Baptism and Eucharist without ministry are only smug expressions of churchly narcissism."

        What does the author mean by these statements? Do you agree or not? Why?

CONCLUDING THE SESSION

- Sing or read in unison "Baptized in Water," no. 492 in *The Presbyterian Hymnal.* Conclude with a time for the participants to reflect on the readings and the five-session study. Remind the group that five daily readings remain in the book. (This might be the time to decide whether the group will meet an additional time following Day 40.) Encourage group members to share what has been most memorable about the study and to offer words of gratitude to one another. Conclude with a prayer.

NOTES: